Cooking For Your D...

Recipes to help ensure a happy childhood
and a healthy future.

Cooking For Your

DIABETIC

Child

Recipes for Children, that **ALL** the
Family will Enjoy!

Sue Hall

THORSONS PUBLISHING GROUP

First published in 1988

© SUE HALL 1988

Illustrations by Juliet Breese

British Library Cataloguing in Publication Data

Hall, Sue, *1962-*
Cooking for your diabetic child: recipes
for healthy eating with children.
1. Diabetes in children—Diet therapy—
Recipes
I. Title
641.5'6314   RJ420.D5

ISBN 0-7225-1586-3

*Published by Thorsons Publishers Limited,
Wellingborough, Northamptonshire, NN8 2RQ, England*

Printed in Great Britain by Richard Clay Limited,
Bungay, Suffolk

3 5 7 9 10 8 6 4 2

Contents

Acknowledgements

The author would like to acknowledge the help and encouragement of Andy, the tasting skills of Henry (aged 1) and Philippa (aged 6)!, and the many children she has worked with at British Diabetic Association Camp who inspired this book.

Recipes
Throughout the book I have used this standard conversion chart:

Weights
25g — 1 oz
50g — 2 oz
75g — 3 oz
100g — 4 oz
150g — 5 oz
175g — 6 oz
200g — 7 oz
225g — 8 oz
250g — 9 oz
275g — 10 oz
300g — 11 oz
350g — 12 oz
375g — 13 oz
400g — 14 oz
425g — 15 oz
450g — 16 oz

Liquid Measures
150ml — ¼ pint
275ml — ½ pint
425ml — ¾ pint
550ml — 1 pint

Spoon Measures
1 teaspoon — 5ml
1 dessertspoon — 10ml
1 tablespoon — 15ml

It is best to use this to get accurate results.

Comparative Oven Temperatures are given below:

Oven Temperatures

Fahrenheit	Centigrade	Gas
300°	150°	No 2
325°	160°	No 3
350°	180°	No 4
375°	190°	No 5
400°	200°	No 6
425°	220°	No 7
450°	230°	No 8

Introduction

We all want to give children the best start in life but we are so bombarded by 'advice' from the media, health professionals and grannies(!) that it is difficult to know where to start.

A child with diabetes could seem to present an even greater problem. However, this need not be so. In diabetes we are aiming for a high-fibre, reduced-fat, low-sugar diet which, of course, is just what everyone is supposed to be chasing in their pursuit of a healthy diet. A diabetic child's prescribed diet can actually make good healthy eating sense. More details of the special nutritional requirements of children are given in Chapter 1.

Diabetes needs special care and attention in all of us — adults and children. Diabetics on insulin (as children will be) should consider carbohydrate and calories — those who have been given an allowance of carbohydrate or calories really should try to stick to it. Everyone with diabetes should see a dietitian regularly — especially children and young people whose food needs change so rapidly. If your child has not seen a dietitian recently or is struggling to keep to his food allowance, now is the time to go back to the clinic. Too often at the British Diabetic Association Camp we meet children of ten or eleven who are still following a food plan given to them at diagnosis age five or six. A dietitian can tailor the diet to your needs and give you the help and support you deserve.

Understanding your child's diabetes and in time helping him to understand it is vital if you are to achieve good control, help your child to stay healthy and get the most out of your life with diabetes. Your child's diet is as important as his insulin or exercise in keeping his blood sugar (glucose) levels down. The purpose of this book, then, is to help you as a family to choose foods wisely and well, thus keeping to a healthy high-fibre, reduced-fat, low-sugar diet. In the reading list on page 104 you will find useful references to books which explain more about diabetes and its control.

More about a Diabetic's Food Plan

Why is so much emphasis placed on fibre and fat? A high fibre intake is good for everyone's general health, it is a natural way to avoid constipation in children and introducing high-fibre foods early on means they begin to regard these foods as normal (more details in Chapter 1). Fibre is particularly helpful for diabetics in keeping their blood sugar (glucose) levels more stable. High-fibre carbohydrate foods (wholemeal bread, beans, etc.) are digested more slowly and the sugar into which they are broken down is released more slowly into the bloodstream than low-fibre, highly-processed foods. This slower release into the bloodstream helps to prevent the peaks (highs) and troughs (lows and hypos) in blood sugar which can be a problem for the diabetic. Thus, a high-fibre breakfast lasts longer — perhaps until morning break — preventing the worry of a 'hypo' at school, or a high-fibre bedtime snack can make a night-time 'hypo' less likely.

Does breakfast in your house look like this?

    Fruit Juice
    Rice Krispies
    Milk
    White toast and butter
    Tea

Try changing it to:

    Fruit juice
    Weetabix
    Milk
    Wholemeal toast and polyunsaturated margarine
    Tea

Just a few simple changes help to increase the fibre intake without affecting carbohydrate intake, if planned properly.

Selecting a diet with less fat is healthier for everyone because of the connection between fat and heart-disease. Heart-disease may seem a long way off in childhood but there is evidence that many children lay the foundations of future problems during their early years. Also establishing healthy habits towards fat now is easier than making major changes later. Special notes about just how much fat to include and why children still need some are in Chapter 1.

These recipes are therefore designed to be as high in fibre and low in fat as possible and can be fitted into most food plans. Your child's diet or eating plan will no doubt emphasize the quantities of the foods they need to eat but the quality of the food is just as important.

Choosing Foods for your Child

It is best to think of foods in three groups:

a) **best choices** i.e., high-fibre, low-fat, low-sugar. These should make up most of a meal and are foods like: wholemeal or wholewheat bread, wholegrain pasta, brown rice, fruit and vegetables, lean meat, fish, low-fat spreads or polyunsaturated margarine, low-fat cheese, semi-skimmed milk.

b) **satisfactory choices** i.e., not too much fat or sugar. These should be used with care and not as often as the above foods. They are things like: white bread, prepared pies, pasties, fatty meat, pâtés, butter, nuts, full-fat dairy products.

c) **poor choices** i.e., low-fibre, high-fat or high-sugar. These should be avoided except in emergencies (e.g. illness or hypoglycaemia — many diabetics use these sugary foods to treat 'hypos' or low blood sugar because they are absorbed quickly by the body) or for very special occasions. They are foods like: sugar, glucose, very sugary foods, sweets, chocolate, iced cakes, instant desserts, etc.

You can think of your choices for your child as traffic lights if you find it easier. (This system has also been very successfully used

by the British Diabetic Association — see the illustration.)
GREEN *for foods you should use regularly.*
AMBER *for foods you can use with caution.*
RED *for foods which should not be used regularly.*

RED SECTION — STOP
Don't use these foods except on
special occasions.

AMBER SECTION — CAUTION
Use these foods with care and not
as the largest part of the diet.

GREEN SECTION — GO
Use these foods regularly.

There are several basic guidelines which can help us all to make
our diets more healthy. Obviously not all are applicable to very
small babies and toddlers — their special needs are again discussed
in Chapter 1.

1.   Always trim fat from meat, think about reducing the portion
of meat given in many cookery books. A 3-4 oz (75-100g) portion
of raw meat is adequate for most children or young people (very
young children will need less). See if you can manage to cook the
meat in time to let it go cold, so you can skim off any fat which
comes to the surface.

2.   Try not to add fat during cooking. Remember to grill instead
of frying. Use a rack to cook meat in your oven or microwave.

3.   Use skimmed milk in baking and semi-skimmed for sauces,
drinks, etc. Look for skimmed milk cheeses instead of cream
cheeses. Skimmed and semi-skimmed milk have the same
carbohydrate value as whole milk but obviously less fat and fewer
calories.

4.   Choose fats of a vegetable origin, use very little butter. Choose

a polyunsaturated margarine or a low-fat spread instead.

5. Try to use wholemeal flour to thicken your sauces and in your baking and pastry.

6. Try to use brown rice and wholegrain pasta in place of the white varieties.

7. Add cooked or canned beans to casseroles, pies, etc. Every ounce of beans you use adds only 5 grammes of carbohydrate and approximately 25 calories, but they are a very important source of fibre and protein. 5-6 oz (150-175g) of dried beans, soaked and cooked, will replace a large 15 oz (425g) tin of beans. There is no need to worry about beans which mention sugar on their labels (or spend extra house-keeping on 'reduced sugar' varieties!), only a tiny quantity of sugar is used and most of it is lost when you rinse and drain your beans (except for baked beans, of course). Also, the amount of fibre is so beneficial that you do not need to worry about rises in blood sugar. If you are going to use dried beans, remember they must be soaked for at least 8 hours, boiled for 10 minutes and then simmered until tender. Remember: tinned or cooked beans freeze well and keep well in the fridge, as long as they are covered.

8. When you buy tinned fish, choose one tinned in brine or tomato sauce **NOT** oil. When you buy tinned fruit, look for natural juice **NOT** syrup.

About the Recipes

Freezing notes are added to help your planning. All spoon measures are level and you should use *either* the Imperial *or* the Metric measurements, not mix the two. All recipes are, of course, thoroughly tried and tested several times. Some of the recipes use ingredients you may not have met before, so the following notes may be helpful.

Flour

a) *Wholemeal and Wholemeal Self-Raising*. These are 100 per cent wholemeal flours made from the whole grain. They contain lots of fibre and are very useful for baking and for use in sauces. They also make good pastry (especially in a food processor). The self raising version must be used if it is specified in a recipe.

(b) *81 per cent Plain and Self-Raising.* The figure 81 per cent refers to the extraction rate of the flour during milling, ie. the amount of grain left in the flour. These therefore contain less fibre than wholemeal but more than white, which has a 70-75 per cent extraction rate. They are a good compromise choice and often produce lighter results than wholemeal versions. If a recipe specifie 81 per cent then this should be used. You will affect the result and of course, the figures by changing around flours in recipes. These flours are made by several companies and are available in health food shops and many supermarkets.

Fructose (Fruit Sugar)
This is a bulk sweetener sold under the brand names of 'Dietade or 'Frusiana'. In these recipes I have followed normal BDA policy of not counting the carbohydrate so long as one does not have more than 1 oz (25g) per day.

1. About Feeding Children

Should Diabetic Children Follow a 'Diabetic' Diet?
Many of the current dietary guidelines for diabetics are very generalized and have been written for the whole diabetic population. Parents often worry about applying these adult guidelines to their diabetic children. Growing children do, of course, have special needs but they should in principle follow the high-fibre, reduced-fat, low-sugar diet; however, there are special cases we need to consider:

1. *Babies*, i.e., 0–2 years.
Diabetic babies need very careful dietary management and their food should be discussed with your dietitian and doctor. Many of the recipes here will be suitable for use but you should always check first. Babies should *not* be given skimmed milk. They need the calories and vitamins found in whole or breast milk. Although fibre is important to small children and now is a good age to introduce healthy eating habits, very small children have fairly small appetites and you must be careful not to provide so much bulk that children are not eating their protein foods and fruit and vegetables. Again, discuss this question with your dietitian. Commercial baby food can also be used of course and the carbohydrate and calorie values of these foods are given in *Countdown* (see Recommended Reading page 104. An actual food allowance will be worked out for you by your doctor or dietitian.

2. *Toddlers/Young Children*, i.e., 2–5 years.
During these years children are forming their eating patterns for life, and it is therefore important to set good standards now. Children should be encouraged to eat a varied diet and to gradually have more high-fibre foods (eg. brown rice, brown bread, etc). It is also

possible to begin to introduce reduced-fat products now such as low-fat yogurt.

However, children under five should still be drinking whole milk and still need lots of calories to grow and 'rush about'. Diabetic children often have between-meal snacks and at this age these can be fairly high energy, eg. dried fruit, high-fibre biscuits, because they will probably be very active. Discuss with your dietitian food changes for special occasions, eg. playgroup. An actual food allowance will be worked out for you by your doctor or dietitian.

3. *At School*
Starting school is a big change in a child's life and for a parent it is often the first time the child has been out of their care for a whole day. If your child is diabetic this can seem an even more daunting prospect. Handing over care to a teacher and meal times to a 'Dinner Lady' are not easy but can be managed successfully. Often the diabetes liaison nurse or dietitian will be willing to contact the school for you to discuss management of diabetes at school.

The British Diabetic Association produce a very useful school pack (see Recommended Reading, page 104) which can help a lot. It must be stressed to your child's teacher that snacks are important and excitement such as games or a new class full of friends can lead to a need for more food (exercise and excitement in some children lowers blood-sugar tremendously).

What to do about lunch at school often becomes a major worry during the lead up to starting school. There are really three options:

(a) *Bring your child home for lunch*. If this is possible, it is perhaps the least traumatic at first. However, it can be a dreadful rush to get them home, fed and back in an hour. For many people, of course, having their child home for lunch is impossible and so they must follow one of the other options.

(b) *Packed Lunch*. Many schools provide facilities for children to eat packed lunch. Packing your own lunch does mean, of course, you can control carbohydrate levels and the types of food offered. The problem is that you're not there to ensure it is all eaten. Using the suggestions here you can produce interesting and nutritious lunches but someone at school must be briefed to check what is being thrown away or staying in the lunch box. Be careful about packing several alternatives in case your child does not feel like something. He may eat the whole lot without realizing the implications for carbohydrate intake. It is important to realize though, that hundreds of diabetic children every day manage very well at school.

(c) *School Lunches.* You may prefer your child to stay for school lunch. Some schools offer a set meal which means you can offer some guidance to the staff as to how much food to serve each day and leave the rest to them. It is slightly more complicated if the school operates a canteen or choice system. An older child will obviously be able to select her own food but young children may be baffled by an array of doughnuts and chips. Often the dining room staff will be only too willing to guide your child if you supply them with the necessary information. Again, it is often invaluable to arrange a visit to the school by the diabetes liaison nurse or the dietitian. This may all sound very daunting but remember many families are coping very well and your doctor, dietitian and nurse are there to help.

4. *Games, P.E. and Swimming*

Views on how to cope with exercise differ so you must discuss this with your own doctor or dietitian. Many children need extra food to combat the lowering of blood-sugar (glucose) levels caused by exercise. There are two ways of dealing with this:

(a) Extra food (carbohydrate) at the meal or snack before the activity.

(b) A special, extra snack or treat just before the activity. Some people feel this encourages people to use chocolate, etc. more than is necessary.

It is important to realize too, that needs will be very individual — a child who swims 20 lengths will use a lot more energy than one who swims two. There is also considerable evidence that a higher fibre, longer lasting carbohydrate given in circumstances (a) above, is more valuable than a quick burst of carbohydrate from a quicker acting snack (eg. chocolate) in (b). Your own dietitian will be able to advise you but it is really a case of finding what best suits your child. Often the blood sugar lowering effects do not become apparent until several hours later. A seemingly unexplained bedtime hypo after a long football match in the morning may well be due to the exercise. It is also worth discussing with your doctor the possibility of altering insulin doses when exercise is anticipated.

5. *Parties*

Parties are designed to be enjoyed by all children and young diabetics should be no exception. A child who is packed off to a party with a great list of 'don't eat . . .' is not going to relax and be happy.

Bearing in mind the extra carbohydrate required to combat exercise and excitement it is probably best to lift all restrictions on very special occasions. Many children are so busy having fun at parties that they eat a lot less 'sugary food' than we fear. Obviously while your child is very young you will be accompanying him anyway, and so will have some control over his intake. Your hostess may well seek advice from you on how to cope with your child and it is probably worth suggesting low-calorie (sugar-free) squash for everyone and leaving it at that. Above all, your child must feel 'normal' and part of the party.

What does a child need to eat?

People often worry about their children eating a balanced diet — with diabetic children it is all too easy to get so focused on carbohydrates that other nutrients are forgotten. How many times have you said 'Eat your potatoes first' or 'Never mind the vegetables, eat your pastry'. We all do it but is it wise?

The vast majority of children in this country are very well fed but it does sometimes help to know about the nutritional content of foods, not so you can analyse each plateful, but so you can keep balanced meals in the back of your mind.

Protein

We all need protein to build new cells and repair damaged ones.

Children of course have a high demand for new cells as they grow and so protein is important to them. Foods containing valuable amounts of protein include:

1. Milk — breast, cow's, goat's and soya.
2. Dairy products, e.g., hard cheese, cottage cheese, butter.
3. Eggs.
4. Soya products.
5. Meat, fish, poultry.
7. Cereal products, e.g., flour, bread, breakfast cereal, oatmeal.
8. Nuts.

As you can see this is quite a wide range of foods. If your child is eating a selection of these foods everyday they will almost certainly be receiving an adequate protein intake. Your dietitian will be able to help more specifically if you are concerned. Protein does contain calories.

Fat

As already discussed in the Introduction, the current nutritional guidelines for adults are to cut down fat in the diet. This guideline however, has to be adapted for children. Fat is a valuable source of energy (calories) which children need to grow. Cutting down too much means children may not be able to eat enough calories. That is why the recipes here use semi-skimmed milk NOT skimmed and margarine NOT low-fat spread. Children should drink whole NOT skimmed milk. Fat is also a carrier for several vitamins (A, D, E, — see page 21).

Having said all of this, too much fat will cause children to put on weight and once a child is over 5, it is worth beginning to control intake. Your own dietitian will help you make this adjustment.

Foods which contain fat include:

1. Milk — breast, cow's, goat's and soya.
2. Eggs.
3. Meat, fish, poultry.
4. Butter, cream, cheese.

5.   Margarine and cooking fats.
6.   Nuts.
7.   Convenience foods, eg. cakes, ice-cream, have fat added.
8   Pastry products.

Carbohydrate
Diabetic families often understand the role of carbohydrate foods in diabetes without applying this to everyday nutrition. Is carbohydrate a 'hypo stopper' in your house or an important part of a child's daily food plan?

Carbohydrate foods provide energy in our diet and bulk to fill us up and some provide fibre. They are converted into energy in the body (often thought of as 'sugar' by diabetics). You will no doubt be familiar with the types of foods containing carbohydrate — these include:

1.   Milk — breast, cow's, goat's and soya.
2.   Cereal products, flour, bread — wholemeal and white.
3.   Pastry products.
4.   Beans, peas, lentils, vegetables.
5.   Fruit.
6.   Nuts.
7.   Sugar — sugary drinks, honey, syrup, etc.
8.   Pasta and pasta products.

There are of course more but no doubt your dietitian will have provided a comprehensive list. The fibre contents of carbohydrate foods obviously differ and wholegrain or wholewheat products obviously contain most — see Introduction.

Vitamins
These are needed for growth, tissue repair and regulating our metabolism. As many of these cannot be made in the body from other foods it is important we eat an adequate supply.

Vitamin A Fat soluble (see section on Fats, page 19), needed for healthy skin and a healthy retina (at the back of the eye). *Sources*

Carrots, green vegetables, dried fruits, liver, dairy products, eg. cheese, butter, milk, eggs and fortified margarine.

Vitamin D Fat soluble (see section on Fats, page 19), needed for absorption of calcium (see below) to produce healthy bones and teeth. Some is produced by the action of the sun on the skin but children need a fairly high intake. *Sources* Dairy products, eg. milk, cheese, butter, cream, fortified margarines, eggs, evaporated milk, liver; fish, e.g. herrings, tinned sardines.

Vitamin E Fat soluble, needed for wound healing and cell repair. *Sources* Cooking fats, wholemeal flour, eggs, nuts.

Vitamin B Water soluble. This is actually a group of vitamins but many foods contain most of them. Needed for digestive system and formation of red blood cells. *Sources* Yeast extract, soya flour, nuts, wholemeal flour and bread, oatmeal, fruit, vegetables and fortified breakfast cereals (these can be an important source for children).

Vitamin C Water soluble, needed for cell growth and maintenance, especially gums and skin, resistance to infection and absorption of iron. *Sources* Citrus fruits, red and green peppers, blackcurrants, green vegetables, potatoes, fresh fruit juice (especially freshly squeezed fruit juice).

Minerals
Only needed in fairly small amounts, these are also an important part of our diet. Some have special relevance to children, eg. calcium. Perhaps the two most important are:

Calcium See Vitamin D section, (above). Needed for healthy bones and teeth. *Sources* Cheese, milk, egg yolk, soya products, nuts, yogurt, fish (especially tinned, eg. sardines).

Iron Needed for healthy blood cells and oxygen transport. *Sources* Bran, soya flour, egg yolk, yeast extract, offal (liver and kidney), dried apricots, wholemeal bread.

This is obviously only a brief summary of food contents and nutrition! Your dietitian will of course be able to supply more details, and discuss your child's actual intake. Also remember many families eat a healthy balanced diet blissfully unaware of vitamins, minerals or proteins so do not worry too much, just try to encourage a varied diet.

2. Healthy Snacks and Lunches

Baked Scotch Eggs

A recipe that avoids deep-fat frying this favourite snack

Makes 2   Total CHO — 50g   Total Cals — 590

---

2 size 3 eggs, hard boiled and shelled
6 oz (175g) low-fat sausagemeat
1 small egg
Pinch of mixed herbs
3 oz (75g) wholemeal breadcrumbs

1. Allow eggs to cool completely.
2. Mix sausagemeat, egg and herbs well. Cover each hard boiled egg with sausagemeat mixture.
3. Roll in breadcrumbs until completely covered.
4. Wrap each 'egg' in foil and bake at 400°F/200°C (Gas Mark 6) for 30 minutes.
5. Remove foil and allow eggs to cool. Serve with salad and rolls or in a packed lunch or picnic.

Each portion contains 25g CHO and 295 calories.

Note: This recipe is *not* suitable for freezing.

Ham and Cheese Calzone

Makes 8 large *or* 16 small
Total CHO — 450g   Total Cals — 2945

1½ lb (675g)
wholemeal flour
Pinch of salt
1 sachet 'fast-acting'
yeast
¾ pint (425ml) tepid
water

Filling
5 oz (150g) strong
cheese, grated
4 oz (100g) lean
boiled ham, chopped
4 tablespoons Tomato
Mix (page 63)

1. Mix flour, salt and yeast.
2. Add water gradually and knead until a soft dough is formed.
3. Knead for 5 minutes. Place in a large bowl, cover with a damp cloth and leave in a warm place until doubled in size (about 1 hour).
4. Divide into 3 oz (75g) pieces (8 in total) or 16 small pieces. Roll each piece into a thin circle. Place on lightly oiled baking trays and cover with a damp cloth.
5. Leave in a warm place to prove (about 15 minutes).
6. Divide tomato mix between circle spreading thinly.
7. Sprinkle on cheese and ham. Fold circles over to form semi-circles and press edges together.
8. Bake at 350°F/180°C (Gas Mark 4) for 20-25 minutes.
9. Allow to cool on a wire rack.

If making 8 each Calzone is 55g CHO and 370 calories.
If making 16 each Calzone is 30g CHO and 185 calories.

Note: This recipe freezes well.

Ham Pizza

Serves 8   Total CHO — 235g   Total Cals — 1400

---

12 oz (350g) wholemeal flour
Pinch of salt
½ sachet 'fast acting' yeast*
⅓ pint (200ml) tepid water
Topping
3 tablespoons Tomato Mix (see page 63)
1½ oz (35g) lean ham (approximately 1½ slices)
2 oz (50g) mushrooms, sliced
2 oz (50g) strong Cheddar cheese, grated

1. Mix flour, salt and yeast.
2. Add water gradually and knead until a soft dough is formed.
3. Knead for 5 minutes. Place in a large bowl, cover with a damp cloth and leave in a warm place until doubled in size (about 1 hour).
4. Knead again for 3 minutes. Press dough into the base of a deep 9-inch (23cm) oiled cake tin or form a 9-inch (23cm) circle on an oiled baking sheet.
5. Cover with a damp cloth and leave in a warm place to prove — about 15 minutes.
6. Spread on Tomato Mix and top with remaining ingredients.
7. Bake at 350°F/180°C (Gas Mark 4) for 30–35 minutes until browned.
8. Serve warm or allow to cool on a wire rack.

Each portion contains 30g CHO and 175 calories.

Note: This recipe freezes well once cooked.

*Because it is easier to use a whole sachet, why not make double quantities of dough and use the other half in another recipe (eg. Salami Pizza, page 26).

Salami Pizza

Serves 8   Total CHO — 235g   Total Cals — 1540

Base
12 oz (350g)
wholemeal flour
Pinch of salt
½ sachet 'fast acting'
yeast*
⅓ pint (200ml) tepid
water

Topping
3 tablespoons Tomato
Mix (page 63)
1½ oz (35g) salami
(approximately 3
slices)
2 oz (50g)
mushrooms, sliced
2 oz (50g) strong
Cheddar cheese,
grated

1. Mix flour, salt and yeast.
2. Add water gradually and knead until a soft dough is formed.
3. Knead for 5 minutes. Place in a large bowl, cover with a damp cloth and leave in a warm place until doubled in size (about 1 hour).
4. Knead again for 3 minutes. Press dough into the base of a deep 9-inch (23cm) oiled cake tin or form a 9-inch (23cm) circle on an oiled baking sheet.
5. Cover with a damp cloth and leave in a warm place to prove — about 15 minutes.
6. Spread on Tomato Mix and top with remaining ingredients.
7. Bake at 350°F/180°C (Gas Mark 4) for 30–35 minutes until browned.
8. Serve warm or allow to cool on a wire rack.

Each portion contains 30g CHO and 190 calories.

Note: This recipe freezes well once cooked.

*Because it is easier to use a whole sachet, why not make double quantities of dough and use the other half in another recipe (eg. Ham Pizza, page 25).

Pancake Parcels

An unusual alternative to sandwiches in a packed lunch

Makes 8   Total CHO — 80g   Total Cals — 520

---

*4 oz (100g)
wholemeal flour
1 size 3 egg
½ pint (275ml) semi-
skimmed milk
Pinch of salt*

1. Beat all ingredients together well until a smooth batter is reached.

2. Allow to stand for 20 minutes.

3. Heat a small heavy based pan and using the minimum of fat, fry 8 pancakes.

4. Stack the pancakes, separated by layers of kitchen paper.

5. Use as required. If they are to be frozen, freeze now, separated by layers of greaseproof paper.

6. Select one of the fillings (see pages 29–30) and fill as required. Serve hot or cold.

Each portion contains 10g CHO and 65 calories.

Note: These pancakes freeze well — EMPTY.

Remember to add the CHO and calories for each pancake to those for your chosen filling.

Pastry Packets
For use with fillings on pages 29-30

Makes 12 packets   Total CHO — 230g   Total Cals — 2335

Pastry
3 oz (75g)
polyunsaturated
margarine
3 oz (75g) white
vegetable fat
12 oz (350g)
wholemeal flour
Pinch of salt
Cold water

1. Rub fats into flour and salt. Mix to a soft dough with cold water.
2. Chill for 15 minutes.
3. Divide into 12 pieces. Roll each to a 3 inch (7cm) circle. Place on lightly oiled baking sheets.
4. Fill as required (see fillings, pages 29-30).
5. Bake at 400°F/200°C (Gas Mark 6) for 30-35 minutes. Allow to cool on a wire rack.

Each pastry piece contains almost 20g CHO and 195 calories.

Note: This pastry freezes well raw. Remember to add filling figures to your share of the pastry.

Fillings
The following can be used in Pancake Parcels (page 27), Pastry Packets (page 28) or Bread Packets (page 36). Remember ALWAYS to add the figures of your filling to whatever base you use.

Chicken and Mushroom

Fills 2 pancakes *or* 4 bread parcels *or* 4 pastry parcels
Total CHO — 15g   Total Cals — 250

3 oz (75g) cooked chicken, diced
2 oz (50g) mushrooms, sliced
¼ pint (150ml) White Sauce (page 63)

1. Mix all ingredients well and allow to cool completely.
2. Use as required, i.e., to fill pancakes, pastry or bread.

Note: This recipe freezes well.

Chicken and Sweetcorn

Fills 2 pancakes *or* 4 bread parcels *or* 4 pastry parcels
Total CHO — 20g   Total Cals — 260

3 oz (75g) cooked chicken, diced
1 oz (25g) sweetcorn, cooked
¼ pint (150ml) White Sauce (page 63)

1. Mix all ingredients well and allow to cool completely.
2. Use as required, i.e., to fill pancakes, pastry or bread.

Note: This recipe freezes well.

Chilli Beef

Fills 3 pancakes *or* 6 bread parcels *or* 6 pastry parcels
Total CHO — 15g   Total Cals 260

4 oz (100g) lean mince Dash of oil 1 small onion, chopped 1 × 5 oz (150g) can tomatoes, chopped Pinch of chilli powder (optional) 2 oz (50g) cooked or tinned kidney beans	**1.** Gently brown the mince in the oil and add the remaining ingredients and stir well. **2.** Bring to the boil and simmer gently for 1 hour. **3.** Allow to cool completely and use as required, i.e. to fill pancakes, pastry or bread. *Note:* This recipe freezes well.

Curried Lentils

Fills 2 pancakes *or* 4 bread parcels *or* 4 pastry parcels
Total CHO — 30g   Total Cals — 165

2 oz (50g) lentils, washed 1 small onion, chopped Seasoning to taste Pinch of curry powder	**1.** Place all ingredients in a small pan with enough water to cover. **2.** Bring to the boil and simmer until lentils are tender and water has been absorbed (approximately 40 minutes). **3.** Allow to cool completely and use as required, i.e. to fill pancakes, pastry or bread. *Note:* This recipe freezes well.

Easy Wholemeal Bread

Makes 2 × 1 lb (450g) loaves
Total CHO — 445g   Total Cals — 2280

½ oz (15g) white
vegetable fat
1½ lb (675g)
wholemeal flour
1 sachet 'fast acting'
yeast
Approximately
¾ pint (425ml)
tepid water

1. Rub fat into flour in a large mixing bowl. Stir in yeast.
2. Add water gradually until a soft dough is formed. Knead for 5 minutes.
3. Return to bowl, cover with a damp cloth and leave in a warm place until doubled in size (approximately 1 hour).
4. Knead again for 2 minutes. Divide mixture into 2 and place in lightly oiled 1 lb (450g) loaf tins. Re-cover and leave until doubled in size (approximately 20 minutes).
5. Bake at 450°F/230°C (Gas Mark 8) for 25-30 minutes.
6. Allow to cool on a wire rack.

Each loaf contains 220g CHO and 1140 calories.

Note: This recipe freezes well.

Open Sandwiches

For 2 slices of bread Total CHO — 25g* Total calories — 305*

2 medium slices wholemeal bread*
1 oz (25g) poly-unsaturated margarine

Cheesy Corn Filling

Total CHO — 15g
Total cals — 225

4 oz (100g) cottage cheese
3 spring onions, chopped
3 oz (75g) sweetcorn, canned or cooked
Seasoning to taste
1 size 3 egg, hard-boiled and chopped

Quarky Peanut Butter Filling

Total CHO — 5g
Total Cals — 210

1 tablespoon peanut butter, bought (or see page 34)
2 oz (50g) quark cheese
1 tablespoon low-fat natural yogurt
Seasoning to taste

1. Spread bread thinly with margarine, cut into triangles.
2. Prepare filling of choice by combining ingredients well.
3. Spread filling onto bread and serve.

Note: Remember to add filling figures to bread figures and divide by number of sandwiches cut. These sandwiches are NOT suitable for freezing.

* Use figures for your usual bread if you prefer.

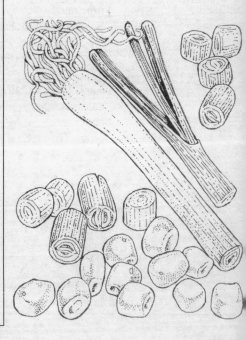

Lunchtime: Doughnut (page 41) and Quarky Peanut Butter Open
Sandwiches (page 32).

A packed lunch: a Chilli Beef Pancake Parcel (page 27) and a Brown Crumpet (page 39), with fresh fruit and a diet drink.

Potato Scones

Makes 16   Total CHO — 145g   Total Cals — 1020

1 lb (450g) potatoes, boiled and mashed (or instant potato to the same quantity)
½ teaspoon salt
2 oz (50g) polyunsaturated margarine
4 oz (100g) wholemeal self-raising flour
½ teaspoon baking powder
A little oil

1. Mix all ingredients well to a soft dough.
2. Form into 16 small balls and flatten with hands.
3. Heat a griddle or heavy based frying-pan and oil lightly.
4. Gently fry each scone for 5 minutes on each side.
5. These scones are best served warm but will keep in an airtight container.

Each scone contains 10g CHO and 65 calories.

Note: This recipe is *not* suitable for freezing.

Peanut Butter

A healthy alternative to the commercial product

Makes 9 oz (250g)   Total CHO — 20g   Total Cals — 1415

---

*8 oz (225g) shelled
peanuts (raw not
roasted)
Pinch of salt
1 fl oz (15ml)
vegetable oil*

1. Skin the peanuts. If this proves difficult, place them on a baking tray in a medium oven for 20 minutes, then place in a dry tea towel and rub well together, then pick nuts out of skins.

2. Place all ingredients in a processor or blender and blend until smooth — about 1 minute.

3. Place in very clean screw top jars. The peanut butter will keep for up to 4 weeks in a fridge.

Note: This recipe is *not* suitable for freezing.

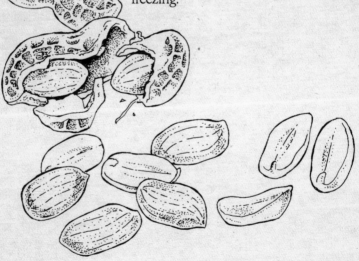

Bread Rolls

What better than your own rolls to pack for a lunch

Makes 14   Total CHO — 445g   Total Cals — 2145

1½ lb (675g)
wholemeal flour
Pinch of salt
1 sachet 'fast acting'
yeast
¾ pint (425ml) tepid
water

1. Mix flour, salt and yeast.

2. Add water gradually and knead until a soft dough is formed.

3. Knead for 5 minutes. Place in a large bowl, cover with a damp cloth and leave in a warm place until doubled in size (about 1 hour).

4. Knead again for 3 minutes. Divide into 14 pieces.

5. Roll pieces into smooth balls and place on lightly-oiled baking sheets.

6. Cover with a damp cloth and leave in a warm place to prove (double in size) for about 20 minutes.

7. Bake at 350°F/180°C (Gas Mark 4) for 15–20 minutes.

8. Allow to cool on a wire rack.

Each roll is 30g CHO and 155 calories.

Note: These rolls freeze well.

Bread Packets

Makes 14   Total CHO — 445g   Total Cals — 2145

*1½ lb (675g)
wholemeal flour
Pinch of salt
1 sachet 'fast acting'
yeast
¾ pint (425ml) tepid
water*

1. Mix flour, salt and yeast.
2. Add water gradually and knead until a soft dough is formed.
3. Knead for 5 minutes. Place in a large bowl, cover with a damp cloth and leave in a warm place until doubled in size (about 1 hour).
4. Knead again for 3 minutes. Divide into 14 pieces.
5. Roll pieces to 5 inch (12cm) circles and place on oiled baking sheets. Cover with a damp cloth and leave in a warm place to prove (about 15 minutes).
6. Fill with chosen filling (pages 29–30). Pull up edges and press together to form triangles or pasty shapes.
7. Bake at 350°F/180°C (Gas Mark 4) for 15 minutes.
8. Allow to cool on a wire rack.

Each portion contains 30g CHO and 155 calories.

Note: This recipe freezes well once cooked. Remember to add the Bread Packet figures to those of your chosen filling.

Tuna and Sweetcorn Roll Up

Slices into 8   Total CHO — 65g   Total Cals — 1520

2 oz (50g)
polyunsaturated
margarine
1 oz (25g) fructose
(fruit sugar)
2 size 3 eggs, beaten
4 oz (100g) wholemeal
self-raising flour
½ teaspoon baking
powder
1 × 7 oz (200g) tin
tuna in brine, drained
3 tablespoons
mayonnaise

1. Cream fat and fructose well, until light and fluffy.
2. Beat in eggs well. Fold in flour and baking powder.
3. Pour into an oiled and lined Swiss roll tin.
4. Bake at 400°F/200°C (Gas Mark 6) for 10–12 minutes.
5. Turn onto greaseproof paper and roll up. Wrap in a damp tea towel until cool.
6. Mix tuna and mayonnaise. Unwrap roll gently and spread with tuna.
7. Re-roll and chill, slice into 8.

Each slice contains about 10g CHO and 190 calories.

Note: This recipe freezes well.

Apricot Shortbread

Cuts into 10   Total CHO — 190g   Total Cals — 2155

8 oz (225g)
wholemeal flour
6 oz (175g)
polyunsaturated
margarine
2 oz (50g) dried
apricots, chopped
1 tablespoon honey
Pinch of salt

1. Mix all ingredients well (preferably in a food processor).
2. Press into a 9 inch (23cm) cake tin and bake at 375°F/190°C (Gas Mark 5) for 35-40 minutes. Mark into 10.
3. Remove from tin and allow to cool on a wire rack.

Each piece contains about 20g and 215 calories.

Note: This recipe freezes well.

Brown Crumpets

Makes 18   Total CHO — 345g   Total Cals — 2254

8 oz (225g) white
flour
8 oz (225g)
wholemeal flour
Pinch of salt
1 sachet 'fast acting'
yeast
3 oz (75g)
polyunsaturated
margarine, melted
1 pint (550ml) semi-
skimmed milk
1 size 3 egg
Vegetable margarine
for frying

1. Mix flours, salt and yeast. Beat in margarine, milk and egg.
2. Beat until a smooth batter is formed.
3. Cover the bowl with a damp cloth and leave in a warm place until doubled in size (about 40 minutes).
4. Lightly grease a griddle or heavy-based frying-pan with vegetable margarine.
5. Pour batter into pan to form smooth circles or use crumpet rings.
6. Cook for 5 minutes each side.
7. Allow to cool on a wire rack. Serve toasted.

Each crumpet contains 20g CHO and 125 calories.

Note: These crumpets freeze well.

Raisin Muffins

Makes 18   Total CHO — 375g   Total Cals — 2010

8 oz (225g) white
flour
8 oz (225g)
wholemeal flour
1 sachet 'fast acting'
yeast
Pinch of salt
½ pint (275ml) semi-
skimmed milk
1 size 3 egg
1 oz (25g)
polyunsaturated
margarine
2 oz (50g) raisins
Vegetable margarine
for frying

1. Mix flours, yeast and salt in a large bowl.
2. Heat milk until lukewarm, beat in egg. Melt margarine and add to milk.
3. Stir raisins into flour. Beat in liquid until a smooth dough is formed.
4. Cover bowl with a damp cloth and leave in a warm place to rise until doubled in size (approximately 40 minutes).
5. Lightly grease a griddle or heavy-based frying-pan with vegetable margarine. Divide dough into 18 pieces, roll into balls and flatten with hands.
6. Allow to cool on a wire rack. Serve split and toasted.

Each muffin (ie. before splitting) contains 20g CHO and 110 calories.

Note: This recipe freezes well.

Doughnuts
A healthier version!

Makes 14   Total CHO — 150g   Total Cals — 1130

---

4 oz (100g) white flour
4 oz (100g) wholemeal flour
Pinch of salt
1 sachet of 'fast acting' yeast
4 tablespoons of semi-skimmed milk
2 oz (50g) polyunsaturated margarine, melted
1 size 3 egg
Vegetable oil for frying

1. Mix flours, salt and yeast. Heat milk to lukewarm and add margarine and egg.
2. Beat liquid into flour until a soft dough is formed.
3. Cover the bowl with a damp cloth and leave in a warm place until doubled in size (about 40 minutes).
4. Turn on to a floured board and knead for 3 minutes. Divide into 14 pieces and shape into rings.
5. Place on a baking sheet and cover with a damp cloth to prove (about 10 minutes).
6. Heat vegetable oil in a saucepan (carefully!) and fry doughnuts for 6 minutes, turning after 3 minutes.
7. Drain well on kitchen paper to remove as much fat as possible.

Each doughnut contains 10g CHO and 80 calories.

Note: This recipe is *not* suitable for freezing.

Mini Mandarin Tarts

For a special occasion add a dash of whipped whipping cream

Makes 14   Total CHO — 135g   Total Cals — 1060

Pastry
2 oz (50g)
polyunsaturated
margarine
6 oz (175g) wholemeal
flour
Cold water

Filling
1 × 10 oz (275g) tin
mandarins in natural
juice
½ teaspoon of
arrowroot

1. Make pastry in the usual way, i.e., rub fat into flour and bring to a *soft* dough with cold water. (The food processor makes excellent wholemeal pastry.)

2. Knead the pastry for 2 minutes and roll out to ⅛ inch (3mm) thick. Using a plain cutter, cut into 14 and line pattie tins. Chill for 10 minutes.

3. Bake cases at 400°F/200°C (Gas Mark 6) for 10 minutes. Remove from tins and allow to cool on a wire rack.

4. Drain the mandarins, saving the juice. Divide the orange segments between the pastry cases.

5. Make the juice up to ⅓ pint (200ml) with water if necessary. Blend in arrowroot. Heat to boiling point, stirring well and remove from heat.

6. Allow to cool until it begins to thicken. Use to glaze the tarts. Allow to cool.

Each tart contains 10g CHO and 75 calories.

Note: This recipe is *not* suitable for freezing but the raw pastry freezes well.

Coconut Tarts

Makes 16   Total CHO — 150g   Total Cals — 2155

Pastry
2 oz (50g)
polyunsaturated
margarine
6 oz (175g) wholemeal
flour
Cold water

Filling
5 oz (150g) desiccated
coconut
2 size 3 eggs, lightly
beaten
8 teaspoons of reduced
sugar jam or fruit
purée

1. Make pastry in the usual way, i.e., rub fat into flour and bring to a *soft* dough with cold water. (The food processor makes excellent wholemeal pastry.)
2. Knead the pastry for 2 minutes and roll out to ⅛ inch (3mm) thick. Using a plain cutter, cut into 16 and line pattie tins. Chill for 10 minutes.
3. Mix coconut and egg well. Place ½ teaspoon of jam in each pastry case and top with coconut mixture.
4. Bake at 400°F/200°C (Gas Mark 6) for 10 minutes or until golden. Allow to cool on a wire rack.

Each tart is about 10g CHO and 135 calories.

Note: This recipe is *not* suitable for freezing but the raw pastry freezes well.

Creamy Orange Jelly

Serves 4   Total CHO — 40g   Total Cals — 240

½ pint (275ml) unsweetened orange juice
1 × 5 oz (150g) carton low-fat natural yogurt
1 sachet gelatine
2 tablespoons boiling water

1. Mix juice and yogurt well.
2. Dissolve gelatine in water and stir into juice mixture.
3. Pour into 4 individual dishes and leave in a cool place to set.

Each portion contains 10g CHO and 60 calories.

Note:This recipe is *not* suitable for freezing.

Home-made Yogurt

Makes 1 pint   Total CHO — 25g   Total Cals — 280

1 pint (550ml) semi-skimmed milk
2 tablespoons low-fat natural yogurt

1. Heat milk to boiling point, boil for 2 minutes, allow to cool to 43°C.
2. Mix into yogurt and place in a special yogurt maker or wide-necked flask.
3. Leave in a warm place for 5 hours.
4. Use kitchen paper to remove water from surface of yogurt. Place in a container and refrigerate until needed.
5. The yogurt will keep for up to 10 days in the fridge.

Note: This recipe is *not* suitable for freezing.

3. Main Courses

Home-made Burgers

Makes 6	Total CHO — neg	Total Cals — 700

12 oz (350g) lean mince
Salt and pepper to taste
1 size 3 egg

1. Mix all ingredients well. Shape into flat rounds.
2. Cover and chill for 15 minutes.
3. Grill for 3 minutes each side to seal and then 10 minutes each side or until cooked through.

Each portion contains negligible CHO and 115 calories.

Note: This recipe freezes well.

Kebabs
An interesting way to introduce vegetables to a child's diet

Serves 4	Total CHO — 10g	Total Cals — 560

12 oz (350g) lean pork fillet in 1 inch (2.5cm) cubes
1 small onion, cut into 8
1 small green pepper, cut into 16
2 tomatoes, cut into 4 pieces each
A little vegetable oil

1. Place alternating pieces of pork and vegetable onto 4 long skewers so that all kebabs are the same.
2. Brush lightly with oil and grill for 4 minutes each side or until the pork is tender.
3. Remove from the skewer to serve since the metal will be hot.

Each kebab contains negligible CHO and 140 calories.

Note: This recipe is not suitable for freezing.

Serve with brown rice and a salad. Remember to add the figures for any accompaniments to your kebab figures.

Spicy Meat Balls

Serves 4   Total CHO — 25g   Total Cals — 665

8 oz (225g) very lean mince
1 medium onion, finely chopped
1 tablespoon vegetable oil
1 tablespoon wholemeal flour
2 teaspoons mixed herbs
Salt and pepper to taste
½ teaspoon chilli powder (optional)
1 medium carrot, chopped
1 × 14 oz (400g) tin tomatoes, chopped

1. Mix mince and ½ the onion well. Form into 16 small balls.
2. Heat the oil in a heavy based pan. Roll balls in the flour and fry gently until brown.
3. Remove balls from pan and reserve.
4. Fry remaining onion and add rest of ingredients. Mix well, bring to the boil and add balls.
5. Cover and simmer gently for 1 hour or place in a casserole and bake at 350°F/180°C (Gas Mark 4) for 1 hour.

Each portion contains approximately 5g CHO and 165 calories.

Note: This recipe freezes well.

Serve with wholegrain pasta or brown rice. Remember to add your rice or pasta figures to the meat balls.

Meat and Bean Loaf

Slices into 4   Total CHO — 65g   Total Cals — 1065

12 oz (350g) lean
mince
1 onion, chopped
1 green pepper,
chopped
1 size 3 egg
Pinch of herbs
½ × 14 oz (400g) tin
Borlotti beans
1 stock cube

1. Combine all ingredients well.
2. Press into a 1 lb (450g) loaf tin. Bake at 350°F/180°C (Gas Mark 4) for 1½ hours.
3. Serve hot or cold.

Each slice contains about 15g CHO and 265 calories.

Note: This recipe freezes well.

Sausage and Egg Cakes

Makes 2   Total CHO — 25g   Total Cals — 240

2 oz (50g) good
quality sausagemeat
1 small egg
Salt and pepper to
taste
2 oz (50g) wholemeal
breadcrumbs

1. Mix sausagemeat and egg well. Season to taste.
2. Shape into flat rounds (like fishcakes) and press into breadcrumbs until well coated.
3. Chill for 15 minutes.
4. Grill for 8 minutes each side.

Serve hot or cold in wholemeal rolls or with jacket potatoes. Remember to add bread or potato figures to your cakes.

Each portion contains between 10-15g CHO and 120 calories.

Note: This recipe freezes well.

Fish Cakes

Makes 4	Total CHO — 60g	Total Cals — 370

5 oz (150g) potato, cooked and mashed
4 oz (100g) white fish fillet, cooked
3 oz (75g) fresh wholemeal breadcrumbs

1. Mix potato and fish well. Form into 4 flat rounds.
2. Coat each fish cake in breadcrumbs and chill for 15 minutes.
3. Grill each fish cake for 5 minutes on each side.

Each fish cake contains 15g CHO and 90 calories.

Note: This recipe freezes well *raw*.

Quick Rissotto

A good way to use left-over cooked rice.

Serves 3	Total CHO — 75g	Total Cals — 610

1 onion, chopped
A little oil
8 oz (225g) cooked brown rice
2 oz (50g) sweetcorn, cooked
2 oz (50g) peas, cooked
1 × 7 oz (200g) tin of tuna in brine, drained

1. Gently fry onion in oil until soft. Add rice and vegetables.
2. Stir well and cook over a medium heat for 5 minutes or until warmed through.
3. Add tuna and cook for 4 minutes. Serve.

Each portion contains 25g CHO and 205 calories.

Note: This recipe is *not* suitable for freezing.

Russian Fish Pie

Serves 4   Total CHO — 170g   Total Cals — 1850

Pastry
8 oz (225g)
wholemeal flour
Pinch of salt
2 oz (50g) white
vegetable fat
2 oz (50g)
polyunsaturated
margarine
Cold water

Filling
6 oz (175g) white fish,
cooked and flaked
3 oz (75g) green peas,
cooked
¼ pint (150ml) White
Sauce (see page
63)

1. Make rough puff pastry by placing flour and salt in a large bowl. Cut fats into walnut-sized pieces and add to flour.
2. Add enough cold water to bring to a soft dough (the fat will still be in pieces).
3. Place on a floured board and roll into a rectangle. Fold the bottom third up and the top third down, turn through 90° and roll again into a rectangle. Repeat this process three times.
4. Chill the pastry for 20 minutes. Meanwhile, mix the filling ingredients.
5. Cut the pastry into 4 equal pieces and roll each to a square (about 5 inches (12cm) square).
6. Place ¼ of the filling on each square. Brush the sides with water and draw up the points to the centre and seal well.
7. Bake at 375°F/190°C (Gas Mark 5) for 15–20 minutes.
8. Serve warm or allow to cool on a wire rack.

Each pie contains 40g CHO and 460 calories.

Note: This recipe is not suitable for freezing, but the raw pastry freezes well.

Potato Fish Pie

Serves 6   Total CHO — 60g   Total Cals — 600

---

8 oz (225g) white fish
fillet, cooked
2 oz (50g)
mushrooms, sliced
½ pint (275ml) White
Sauce (page 63)
5 oz (150g) mashed
potato

1. Flake fish, remove skin and any bones.
2. Mix with mushrooms and sauce.
3. Place in an ovenproof dish and top with potato.
4. Bake at 350°F/180°C (Gas Mark 4) for 25–30 minutes *or* microwave on MEDIUM until warmed through (approximately 5–10 minutes).

Each portion contains 10g CHO and 100 calories.

Note: This recipe freezes well.

Herby Fish

Serves 2   Total CHO — 10g   Total Cals — 230

---

2 cod fillets — about
4 oz (100g) each
1 × 14 oz (400g) tin
tomatoes
3 oz (75g)
mushrooms, sliced
1 medium onion,
chopped
Good-sized pinch of
mixed herbs

1. Place all ingredients in a covered casserole.
2. Bake at 350°F/180°C (Gas Mark 4) for 40 minutes or until fish is cooked through.

Each portion contains 5g CHO and 115 calories.

Serve with brown rice or a jacket potato.

Note: This recipe freezes well.

Eggy Potatoes

Serves 2   Total CHO — 60g   Total Cals — 770

---

*2 × 5 oz (150g)
potatoes
2 size 3 eggs
2 oz (50g)
polyunsaturated
margarine*

1. Wash the potatoes well, prick with a fork and bake at 400°F/200°C (Gas Mark 6) until tender (approximately 1 hour). You can microwave your potatoes; follow your machine's instructions.

2. Once soft, cut out tops. Remove a tablespoonful of potato.

3. Cream margarine into potato and press back into skin.

4. Break 1 egg into each potato and replace top.

5. Heat under grill for 3–4 minutes or until egg is baked.

Each potato contains 30g CHO and 385 calories.

Note: This recipe is *not* suitable for freezing.

Special Macaroni

Serves 4   Total CHO — 115g   Total Cals — 1560

1 × 7 oz (200g) tin pilchards in tomato sauce
6 oz (175g) wholewheat macaroni
1 pint (550ml) White Sauce (page 63)
8 oz (225g) fresh tomato
2 oz (50g) strong cheese, grated

1. Place pilchards and sauce in a flame-proof dish. Cover and place in a low oven to heat through.
2. Meanwhile, cook macaroni in boiling salted water until tender (approximately 15 minutes) and drain well.
3. Stir macaroni into white sauce and pour onto fish.
4. Top with sliced tomato and grated cheese.
5. Brown under a hot grill.

Each portion contains about 30g CHO and 390 calories.

Note: This recipe is *not* suitable for freezing.

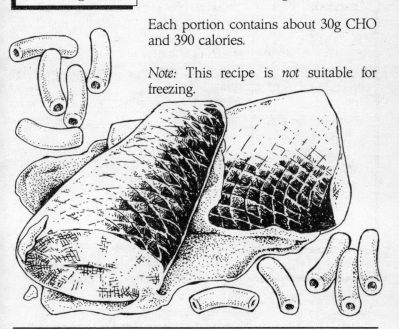

Individual Quiches

Children love to have a little quiche all to themselves.

Makes 6
Pastry: Total CHO 115g   Pastry: Total Cals — 920

Pastry
2 oz (50g)
polyunsaturated
margarine
6 oz (175g) wholemeal
flour
Cold water

**Ham and
Mushroom Filling**

Total CHO — 10g
Total Cals — 260

2 oz (50g)
mushrooms, thinly
sliced
2 oz (50g) lean boiled
ham, chopped
1 size 3 egg
6 tablespoons of semi-
skimmed milk
Salt and pepper to
taste

**Cheese and
Onion Filling**

1. Make pastry in the usual way, i.e., rub fat into flour and bring to a soft dough with cold water. (The food processor makes excellent pastry.)

2. Knead for 2 minutes and roll out to ⅛ inch (3mm) thick. Cut to fit 3-inch (7cm) individual tins or Yorkshire pudding trays, line trays and chill for 10 minutes.

3. Choose filling. Place dry ingredients in base of cases. Mix egg, milk and seasonings well. Carefully pour egg mixture into the cases.

4. Bake at 400°F/200°C (Gas Mark 6) for 15 minutes or until golden and firm to the touch.

5. Serve hot or allow to cool on a wire rack.

Each Ham and Mushroom quiche contains 20g CHO and 195 calories

Each Cheese and Onion quiche contains 20g CHO and 215 calories.

Note: These recipes freeze well. If you do not have individual cases, use the same ingredients to make 1 × 8 inch (20cm) quiche and cut into 6.

Total CHO — 15g
Total Cals — 380

2 oz (50g) strong
    cheese, grated
1 small onion, finely
    chopped
1 size 3 egg
6 tablespoons of semi-
    skimmed milk
Salt and pepper to
    taste

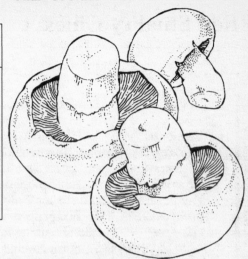

Baked Egg, Cheese and Beans
A tasty, easy meal

Serves 2   Total CHO — 20g   Total Cals — 385

1 × 5 oz (150g) tin
    baked beans
1 size 3 egg, lightly
    beaten
2 oz (50g) strong
    cheese, grated

1. Mix all ingredients well. Pour into a bowl or small casserole dish.
2. Microwave on MEDIUM for 5 minutes or until set *or* bake at 350°F/180°C (Gas Mark 4) for 20-25 minutes or until set.
3. Serve warm.

Each portion contains 10g CHO and 195 calories.

Note: This recipe is *not* suitable for freezing. This is often popular with toddlers served with a finger of brown toast. Remember to add the figures for your toast to those for your beans.

Red Stir-Fry Chicken

Serves 4   Total CHO — 15g   Total Cals — 445

2 tablespoons soya
    sauce
2 chicken breasts —
    about 5 oz (150g)
    each — skinned and
    sliced very thinly
A little oil
4 spring onions,
    chopped
1 onion, chopped
½ red pepper, chopped
½ green pepper,
    chopped
8 oz (225g)
    beansprouts
2 oz (50g)
    mushrooms, sliced
4 oz (100g) red
    cabbage, sliced

1. Mix soya sauce and chicken — leave
to marinate for 20 minutes.
2. Heat oil in a wok or large heavy based
pan. Pour in chicken and sauce. Stir well
and fry for 3 minutes, stirring all the time.
3. Add spring onions and onion — fry
and stir for 2 minutes.
4. Add peppers and stir-fry for 2 minutes.
Add remaining ingredients.
5. Stirring well, fry for 5-7 minutes until
hot through. Serve.

Each portion contains negligible CHO
and 110 calories.

Note: This recipe is not suitable for
freezing.

A morning snack for school: Muesli Drops (page 70) and a banana.

A bedtime snack: a slice of Kolac (page 71) and a glass of milk.

A weekend lunch in a hurry: a Home-made Burger (page 45) and a pot of diet yogurt.

An evening meal: a piece of Ham Pizza (page 25) with salad and a portion of Apricot Queen of Puddings (page 81).

Chinese Choux Buns

Makes 6   Total CHO — 65g   Total Cals — 1310

Choux Pastry
*3 oz (75g)
polyunsaturated
margarine*
¼ pint (150ml) water
*3 oz (75g) wholemeal
flour*
2 size 3 eggs, beaten

Filling
*6 oz (175g) chicken,
cooked and cubed*
*3 oz (75g)
beansprouts*
3 oz (75g) mushrooms
*¼ pint White Sauce
(page 63), cold*

1. In a heavy based pan melt margarine in water. Bring to the boil.

2. Remove from heat and quickly beat in flour until the mixture is glossy and forms a ball which leaves the side of the pan.

3. Beat in eggs until glossy and smooth. Spoon or pipe 6 buns onto a lightly-oiled tray.

4. Bake at 400°F/200°C (Gas Mark 6) for 20 minutes.

5. Cool on a wire rack. While still warm, cut off tops to release steam.

6. Mix all filling ingredients and spoon into cases, replace tops.

Each bun and filling contains about 10g CHO and 220 calories.

Note: This recipe is *not* suitable for freezing.

Sunshine Chicken

Serves 4   Total CHO — 10g   Total Cals — 380

A little oil
10 oz (275g) lean
chicken, cubed
3 oz (75g)
mushrooms, sliced
1 yellow pepper, sliced
into rings
1 medium onion,
chopped
¾ pint (425ml)
chicken stock

1. Heat oil in a heavy based pan and gently fry chicken until lightly browned.
2. Add vegetables, stir well, add stock.
3. Cook at 350°F/180°C (Gas Mark 4) for 1 hour. Serve with brown rice or a jacket potato.

Each portion contains negligible CHO and 95 calories.

Note: This recipe freezes well.

Chicken Nuggets

A healthy alternative to the deep fried ones from the burger shop.

Makes 14   Total CHO — 40   Total Cals — 470

---

1 chicken breast —
about 5 oz (150g)
weight — skinned
1 size 3 egg
4 oz (100g) fresh
wholemeal
breadcrumbs

1. Cut the chicken into 14 equal pieces — about ½ inch (1cm) cubes.
2. Beat the egg lightly and coat each piece of chicken.
3. Coat in breadcrumbs.
4. Grill for 4–5 minutes each side. Allow to cool.

Serve with the Dips on pages 95–7.

Each nugget contains 3g CHO and 35 calories.

Note: These nuggets freeze well.

Wholemeal Pasties

Makes 12   Total CHO — 260g   Total Cals — 2650

Pastry
3 oz (75g)
polyunsaturated
margarine
3 oz (75g) white
vegetable fat
12oz (350g)
wholemeal flour
Pinch of salt
Cold Water

Sauce
¼ pint (150ml) White
Sauce (page 63)
1oz (25g) strong
Cheddar, grated

Filling
1 carrot, grated
1 parsnip, grated
1 leek, grated
1 courgette, finely
chopped

1. Rub fat in flour and salt. Mix to a soft dough with a little cold water. Divide into 12.
2. Roll each piece to a 3 inch (7cm) circle. Place on a baking sheet and chill.
3. Mix the sauce with the Cheddar and add enough to the vegetables to just dampen. Divide the vegetables between the circles, fold over and seal.
4. Bake at 400°F/200°C (Gas Mark 6) for 30-35 minutes. Allow to cool on a wire rack.

Each pastry contains 20g CHO and 220 calories.

Note: This recipe freezes well.

Vegetarian Quiches

Makes 6

Pastry: Total CHO — 115g   Pastry: Total Cals — 920

Pastry
2 oz (50g) vegetable margarine
6 oz (175g) wholemeal flour
Cold water

Mixed Vegetable Filling

Total CHO — 25g
Total Cals — 245

2 oz (50g) mushrooms, thinly sliced
2 oz (50g) cooked lentils
1 small tomato, finely chopped
1 size 3 egg
6 tablespoons of semi-skimmed milk
Sea salt and pepper

Bean and Cheese Filling

Total CHO — 15g

1. Make pastry in the usual way, i.e., rub fat into flour and bring to a soft dough with cold water. (The food processor makes excellent pastry.)

2. Knead for 2 minutes and roll out to ⅛ inch (3mm) thick. Cut to fit 3 inch (7cm) individual tins or Yorkshire pudding trays, line trays and chill for 10 minutes.

3. Choose filling. Place dry ingredients in the base of cases. Mix egg, milk and seasonings well. Carefully pour egg mixture into the cases.

4. Bake at 400°F/200°C (Gas Mark 6) for 15 minutes or until golden and firm to the touch.

5. Serve hot or allow to cool on a wire rack.

Each Mixed Vegetable quiche contains about 25g CHO and 195 calories.

Each Bean and Cheese quiche contains 20g CHO and 220 calories.

Note: These recipes freeze well. If you do not have individual cases, use the same ingredients to make 1 × 8 inch (20cm) quiche and cut into 6.

Total Cals — 400

2 oz (50g) baked
beans, drained well
2 oz (50g) strong
cheese, grated
1 size 3 egg
6 tablespoons of semi-
skimmed milk
Sea salt and pepper

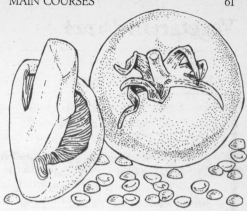

Lentil Bean Loaf

Slices into 8   Total CHO — 170g   Total Cals — 1050

8 oz (225g) green
lentils, washed
1 onion, chopped
½ green pepper,
chopped
1 medium carrot,
chopped
½ × 14oz (400g) tin
Borlotti beans
Pinch of herbs
1 size 3 egg, beaten
1 × 5 oz (150g)
carton low-fat natural
yogurt
1 vegetable stock cube

1. Cook lentils by bringing to the boil and simmering for 30 minutes. Drain well. Allow to cool.

2. Combine all ingredients well. Press into a lightly oiled 2 lb (900g) loaf tin.

3. Bake at 350°F/180°C (Gas Mark 4) for ¾ hour.

4. Serve warm or allow to cool completely.

Each slice is 20g CHO and 130 calories.

Note: This recipe freezes well.

Vegetarian Pizza

Serves 8   Total CHO — 250g   Total Cals — 1210

Base
*12 oz (350g)
wholemeal flour
Pinch of salt
½ sachet 'fast acting'
yeast**
*⅓ pint (200ml) tepid
water*

Topping
*3 tablespoons Tomato
Mix (see page 63)
2 oz (50g)
mushrooms, sliced
½ green pepper,
sliced
2 oz (50g) sweetcorn
1 oz (25g) cooked or
tinned kidney beans*

1. Mix flour, salt and yeast.
2. Add water gradually and knead until a soft dough is formed.
3. Knead for 5 minutes. Place in a large bowl, cover with a damp cloth and leave in a warm place until doubled in size (about 1 hour).
4. Knead again for 3 minutes. Press dough into the base of a deep 9 inch (23cm) oiled cake tin or form a 9 inch (23cm) circle on an oiled baking sheet.
5. Cover with a damp cloth and leave in a warm place to prove — about 15 minutes.
6. Spread on Tomato Mix and top with remaining ingredients.
7. Bake at 350°F/180°C (Gas Mark 4) for 30-35 minutes until browned.
8. Serve warm or allow to cool on a wire rack.

Each portion contains 30g CHO and 150 calories.

Note: This recipe freezes well once cooked.

* Because it is easier to use a whole sachet, why not make double quantities of dough and use the other half in another recipe (e.g. Ham Pizza page 25).

White Sauce

Makes 1 pint (550ml)   Total CHO — 60g   Total Cals — 600

---

*1 pint (550ml) semi-skimmed milk
2 oz (50g) wholemeal flour
1 oz (25g) polyunsaturated margarine, chopped
Seasoning to taste*

1. Place all ingredients in a saucepan. Stir well.
2. Heat to boiling, stirring ALL the time.
3. Reduce heat and simmer for 2 minutes.
4. Use as required.

Note: This recipe is *not* suitable for freezing except in made up dishes (e.g. Wholemeal Pasties page 59).

Tomato Mix

For use in Ham Pizza (page 25), etc.

Makes ⅓ pint (200ml)   Total CHO — 10g   Total Cals — 45

---

*1 small onion, chopped
1 teaspoon oregano
5 medium fresh tomatoes or 5 tinned tomatoes, drained*

1. Place all ingredients in a blender or liquidizer and process until very fine and smooth.

or

1. Chop all ingredients well and mix until smooth.
2. Use as required.

Note: This recipe freezes well.

4. Baking and Puddings

Cheese Scones

Makes 16   Total CHO — 160g   Total Cals — 1370

2 oz (50g)
polyunsaturated
margarine
8 oz (225g) 81% self-
raising flour
2 oz (50g) strong
cheese, grated
¼ pint (150ml) semi-
skimmed milk

1. Rub fat into flour, add cheese, stir in milk. Knead to a smooth dough.
2. Roll out to ½ inch (1cm) thick. Cut into 16. Place on a baking sheet.
3. Bake at 425°F/220°C (Gas Mark 7) for 25 minutes. Allow to cool on a wire rack.

Each scone contains 10g CHO and 85 calories.

Note: This recipe freezes well.

American Corn Bread

Cuts into 14   Total CHO — 210g   Total Cals — 1545

6 oz (175g) corn meal
or maize flour
4 oz (100g)
wholemeal self-raising
flour
2 teaspoons baking
powder

1. Mix corn meal, flour, baking powder and salt.
2. Rub in margarine. Beat milk and egg together, pour into dry mixture and beat well.
3. Pour into a lightly oiled 7 inch (18cm) square cake tin.

1 teaspoon salt
2 oz (50g)
polyunsaturated
margarine
½ pint (275ml) semi-
skimmed milk
1 size 3 egg

4. Bake at 400°F/200°C (Gas Mark 6) for 25–30 minutes.
5. Leave to cool in tin for 5 minutes then on a wire rack. Serve with savoury dishes, such as chicken or spread with margarine and low-sugar jam.

Each slice contains 15g CHO and 110 calories.

Note: This recipe freezes well.

Marbled Carob Cake

Slices into 8   Total CHO — 70g   Total Cals — 1320

4 oz (100g)
wholemeal self-raising
flour
1 teaspoon baking
powder
4 oz (100g)
polyunsaturated
margarine
1 oz (25g) fructose
(fruit sugar)
2 size 3 eggs
1 dessertspoon carob
2 tablespoons semi-
skimmed milk

1. Place all ingredients *except* carob in a bowl and beat well together (a food processor works well).
2. Divide the mixture into 2 equal portions.
3. Add carob to one of the portions, therefore producing 2 colours of mixture.
4. Place alternating tablespoonfuls of white and brown mixture into a lightly oiled 1 lb (450g) loaf tin.
5. Bake at 350°F/180°C (Gas Mark 4) for 30–40 minutes or until springy to the touch.
6. Allow to cool on a wire rack.

Each slice contains almost 10g CHO and 165 calories.

Note: This recipe freezes well.

Pear Sponges

Makes 24   Total CHO — 125g   Total Cals — 2295

6 oz (175g)
wholemeal self-raising
flour
1½ teaspoons baking
powder
6 oz (175g)
polyunsaturated
margarine
2 oz (50g) fructose
(fruit sugar)
3 size 3 eggs
2 pear halves — fresh
peeled or tinned in
natural juice

1. Place all ingredients in a bowl and beat well together (a processor works well here).
2. Spoon into 24 paper cases or bun tins.
3. Bake at 350°F/180°C (Gas Mark 4) for 8-10 minutes until golden brown and springy.
4. Allow to cool on a wire rack.

Each sponge contains 5g CHO and 95 calories.

Note: This recipe freezes well.

Apricot Choux Buns

Makes 8   Total CHO — 85g   Total Cals — 1570

Choux Pastry
3 oz (75g)
polyunsaturated
margarine
¼ pint (150ml) water
3 oz (75g) wholemeal
flour
2 size 3 eggs, beaten

1. In a heavy-based pan melt margarine in water. Bring to the boil.
2. Remove from heat and quickly beat in flour until it is glossy and forms a ball which leaves the side of the pan.
3. Beat in eggs until glossy and smooth. Spoon or pipe in 8 pieces on a lightly-oiled tray.
4. Bake at 400°F/200°C (Gas Mark 6) for 15 minutes.

Filling
2 oz (50g) dried
apricots, soaked and
stewed
1 × 5 oz (150g)
carton low-fat sugar-
free apricot yogurt
¼ pint (150ml)
whipping cream

5. Cool on a wire rack. While still warm, cut off tops to release steam.
6. Mix apricots and yogurt. Whip cream and fold gently into fruit. Fill cases. Replace tops.

Each bun contains 10g CHO and 200 calories.

Note: This recipe is *not* suitable for freezing.

Potato Sultana Scones

Makes 12   Total CHO — 180g   Total Cals — 1210

2 oz (50g)
polyunsaturated
margarine
6 oz (175g)
wholemeal self-raising
flour
2 oz (50g) potato,
cooked, mashed, cold
3 oz (75g) sultanas
¼ pint (150ml) semi-
skimmed milk

1. Rub margarine into flour. Stir in potato and sultanas. Mix to a soft dough with milk.
2. Roll out to ½ inch (1cm) thick and cut into 12.
3. Place on a baking sheet and bake at 400°F/200°C (Gas Mark 6) for 20-25 minutes.
4. Allow to cool on a wire rack.

Each scone contains 15g CHO and 100 calories.

Note: this recipe freezes well.

Bannocks (Scottish Oat Cakes)

Makes 16   Total CHO — 160g   Total Cals — 1245

7 oz (200g) oatmeal
— or oats
1 oz (25g) wholemeal
flour
½ teaspoon salt
½ teaspoon baking
powder
2 oz (50g)
polyunsaturated
margarine
6 tablespoons hot
water
A little oil

1. If using oats, blend them in a processor or blender for a few seconds until finer.
2. Mix oatmeal, flour, salt, and baking powder. Rub in margarine.
3. Stir in hot water until a smooth dough is formed. Divide into 16 equal pieces. Roll out to thin circles.
4. Heat a griddle or heavy based frying-pan and oil lightly.
5. Fry each bannock for 5 minutes on each side and allow to cool on a wire rack.

Each bannock is 10g CHO and 80 calories.

Note: This recipe freezes well.

Peanut Biscuits

Makes 14   Total CHO — 70g   Total Cals — 1070

2 oz (50g) Peanut
Butter (page 34)
2 oz (50g) margarine
2 teaspoons fructose
(fruit sugar)
1 size 3 egg
4 oz (100g)
wholemeal self-raising
flour

1. Cream peanut butter and margarine until fluffy.
2. Stir in fruit sugar and egg. Add flour. Mix well.
3. Roll into 14 small balls, flatten with your hands. Place on a lightly-oiled baking tray.
4. Bake at 350°F/180°C (Gas Mark 4) for 15 minutes until golden brown.
5. Allow to cool on a wire rack.

Each biscuit contains 5g CHO and 75 calories.

Note: This recipe freezes well.

Lemony Date Scones

Cuts into 12   Total CHO — 185g   Total Cals — 1080

2 oz (50g) dried, stoned dates, chopped
Juice and rind of 1 lemon
8 oz (225g) wholemeal self-raising flour
1 teaspoon baking powder
1 oz (25g) polyunsaturated margarine
¼ pint (150ml) semi-skimmed milk

1. Soak dates in juice and rind for 1 hour.
2. Mix flour and baking powder, rub in margarine. Add milk and fruit mixture. Mix to a soft dough.
3. Knead to a circle 1 inch (2cm) thick. Mark into 12. Place on a baking tray. Bake at 350°F/180°C (Gas Mark 4) for 20-30 minutes.
4. Allow to cool on a wire rack.

Each piece contains 15g CHO and 90 calories.

Note: This recipe freezes well.

Muesli Drops

Makes 24   Total CHO — 100g   Total Cals — 890

---

2 oz (50g) polyunsaturated margarine
½ tablespoon golden syrup
3 oz (75g) unsweetened muesli
2 oz (50g) wholemeal flour
½ teaspoon bicarbonate of soda
Boiling water

1. Melt margarine and syrup in a heavy based pan, remove from heat.
2. Mix bicarbonate of soda into 1 tablespoon of boiling water. Stir into fat.
3. Mix in all remaining ingredients. Beat well.
4. Drop teaspoons on to a lightly oiled tray, leaving 1½ inches (4cm) between spoonfuls.
5. Bake at 300°F/150°C (Gas Mark 2) for 15–20 minutes. Leave on the tray for 2 minutes. Allow to cool on a wire rack.
6. Always store in an airtight container.

Each drop contains 5g CHO and 40 calories.

Note: This recipe is not suitable for freezing.

Kolac

An interesting 'different' biscuit

Slices into 24   Total CHO — 235g   Total Cals — 2550

---

8 oz (225g)
wholemeal flour
2 teaspoons baking
powder
½ teaspoon salt
5 oz (150g)
polyunsaturated
margarine
1 size 3 egg
2 medium bananas,
sliced
4 oz (100g) stoned
dates, chopped
12 oz (350g) cottage
cheese

1. Mix flour, baking powder and salt. Rub in fat and beat in egg.

2. Use your hands to bring the dough together.

3. Roll out to fit a lightly oiled Swiss roll tin. Press in.

4. Top with bananas, dates and cottage cheese.

5. Bake at 400°F/200°C (Gas Mark 6) for 30 minutes.

6. Allow to cool in the tin before slicing.

Each slice contains 10g CHO and 105 calories.

Note: This recipe is *not* suitable for freezing.

Chewy Date Sponges

Makes 16   Total CHO — 245g   Total Cals — 1675

6 oz (175g)
*wholemeal self-raising
flour*
Pinch of salt
3 oz (75g)
*polyunsaturated
margarine*
5 oz (150g) stoned
dates, chopped
2 tablespoons orange
juice
2 oz (50g) raisins
1 size 3 egg
2 tablespoons semi-
skimmed milk
½ teaspoon mixed
spice

1. Beat or process all ingredients well.
2. Turn into a lightly oiled Swiss roll tin.
3. Bake at 350°F/180°C (Gas Mark 4) for 30–40 minutes. Allow to cool in the tin. Cut into 16.

Each square contains 15g CHO and 105 calories.

Note: This recipe freezes well.

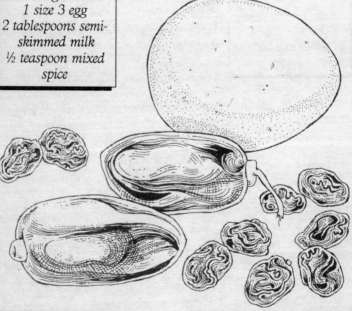

Prunes in a Hole

A sweet variation on Toad in the Hole.

Makes 24   Total CHO — 160g   Total Cals — 845

---

24 dried, stoned
prunes —
approximately 7 oz
(200g) — soaked
4 oz (100g)
wholemeal flour
1 large egg
½ pint (275ml) semi-
skimmed milk

1. Drain the prunes, place one in the base of each of 24 bun cases or Yorkshire pudding tins.
2. Beat flour, egg and milk together well. Leave to stand for 10 minutes.
3. Share the batter between the 24 cases.
4. Bake at 400°F/200°C (Gas Mark 6) for 20 minutes.
5. Allow to cool on a wire rack.

Each 'hole' contains about 5g CHO and 35 calories.

Note: This recipe is *not* suitable for freezing.

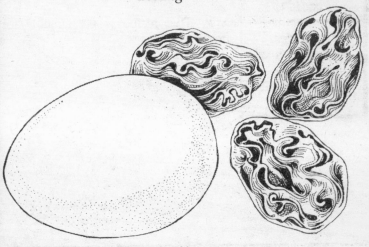

Prune and Walnut Squares

Makes 14   Total CHO — 220g   Total Cals 2160

Topping
1 × 15 oz (425g) tin
prunes in natural
juice
1 oz (25g)
polyunsaturated
margarine
¼ teaspoon cinnamon
2 oz (50g) walnuts

Cake
8 oz (225g)
wholemeal flour
1 teaspoon baking
powder
Pinch of salt
4 oz (100g)
polyunsaturated
margarine
Juice from tinned
prunes made up to ½
pint (275ml) with
water

1. Drain the prunes, keeping the juice for the cake, stone them and set aside.
2. Melt the margarine, stir in cinnamon and walnuts and set aside.
3. Beat all cake ingredients together well (a processor is ideal).
4. Pour into a lightly oiled 8 inch (20cm) cake tin. Top with prunes, nuts and margarine.
5. Bake at 350°F/180°C (Gas Mark 5) for 45 minutes.
6. Allow to cool in the tin. Best served the day it is made.

Each slice contains 15g CHO and 155 calories.

Note: This recipe is not suitable for freezing.

Rhubarb Ice Cream

Serves 6   Total CHO — 40g   Total Cals — 780

---

1 lb (450g) rhubarb
½ pint (275ml) water
2 oz (50g) stoned
dates
1 size 3 egg
2 size 3 egg yolks
1 × 5 oz (150g)
carton of whipping
cream

1. Wash and chop the rhubarb, place in a saucepan with the water. Bring to the boil, add the dates and simmer until the rhubarb is tender.

2. Drain the rhubarb and dates, reserving juice, purée them and set them aside to cool.

3. Boil the juice left from boiling the fruit for 1 minute.

4. In a blender or processor beat the egg and egg yolks until creamy. On high speed pour the boiling syrup into the processor or blender, and beat for 2-3 minutes until thick and moussey.

5. Gently fold in the fruit purée and cream.

6. Pour into an ice cream machine *or* a foil container and place in the freezer. (The freezer compartment of the fridge will do.) As the mixture freezes, stir it 2 or 3 times.

7. Once frozen, process, blend or whisk the ice cream until smooth.

8. Take out of the freezer for 10 minutes before serving.

Each portion contains about 5g CHO and 130 calories.

Apple and Blackberry Packets

Makes 2   Total CHO — 30g   Total Cals 680

8 oz (225g)
blackberries, washed
½ tablespoon honey
3 oz (75g)
polyunsaturated
margarine
8 oz (225g) cooking
apples — peeled
1 teaspoon cinnamon

1. Place drained blackberries in a bowl, add honey and leave to stand for 2 hours (to bring out juice).
2. Cut two foil squares 8 inches (20cm).
3. Brush foil with a little of the margarine melted.
4. Slice apples thinly and place on foil. Top with blackberries and cinnamon.
5. Dot with remaining margarine and seal foil.
6. Bake at 350°F/180°C (Gas Mark 4) for 40 minutes.

Each packet contains 15g CHO and 340 calories.

Note: This recipe is *not* suitable for freezing.

Rhubarb Crumble Top

Cuts into 8   Total CHO — 195g   Total Cals — 2030

Pastry
*3 oz (75g)
polyunsaturated
margarine
6 oz (175g)
wholemeal flour
Cold water*

Filling
*8 oz (225g) rhubarb
1 oz (25g) dried
apricots, soaked*

Topping
*4 oz (100g)
wholemeal flour
3 oz (75g)
polyunsaturated
margarine*

1. Make pastry in the usual way, i.e., rub fat into flour and bring to a soft dough with the cold water (the food processor makes excellent wholemeal pastry).

2. Roll out and line a 9 inch (23cm) flan dish. Chill for 10 minutes and bake blind at 400°F/200°C (Gas Mark 6) for 15 minutes.

3. Stew the rhubarb and apricots in ⅓ pint (200ml) water. Fill the flan dish with the stewed, mashed fruit.

4. Mix topping ingredients well and place over fruit.

5. Bake at 400°F/200°C (Gas Mark 6) for 25–30 minutes until golden.

6. Serve hot or cold.

Each slice contains 25g CHO and 250 calories.

Note: This recipe freezes well.

Special Microwave Banana Custard

If you do not have a microwave just use conventional custard

Serves 2   Total CHO — 50g   Total Cals — 275

---

1 oz (25g) stoned dates, chopped
½ pint (275ml) semi-skimmed milk
1 medium banana
1 dessertspoon custard powder

1. Mix dates into milk and leave to stand for ½ hour to draw sweetness out of the dates.

2. Drain dates from milk and place in serving dish with peeled sliced banana.

3. Mix custard powder into milk in a large glass or plastic measuring jug. Microwave on HIGH for 2 minutes. Stir well.

4. Microwave on HIGH for 1 minute or until thick and smooth.

5. Pour custard over fruit and serve *or* leave to cool and serve chilled.

Each portion contains 25g CHO and 140 calories.

Note: This recipe is *not* suitable for freezing.

Plum Pudding

Serves 4   Total CHO — 135g   Total Cals — 1175

1½ lb (675g) cooking plums, stoned and halved
6 oz (175g) crustless wholemeal stale bread, sliced
3 oz (75g) polyunsaturated margarine
1 tablespoon golden syrup
2 tablespoons semi-skimmed milk

1. Lightly oil a deep baking dish.
2. Spread the bread on one side with margarine. Line the baking dish, margarine side up — reserving some bread to cover the top.
3. Place plums inside bread. Top with golden syrup. Top with bread and milk.
4. Bake at 375°F/190°C (Gas Mark 5) for 1½ hours.

Each portion contains almost 35g CHO and 295 calories.

Note: This recipe is not suitable for freezing.

Brown Bread Whip

Serves 4   Total CHO — 40g   Total Cals — 1030

¼ pint (150ml) semi-skimmed milk
2 size 3 eggs, separated
½ teaspoon cornflour
2 thick slices wholemeal bread
2 oz (50g) mixed chopped nuts
¼ pint (150ml) whipping cream

1. Place milk in a saucepan and bring to the boil.

2. Beat yolks and cornflour together, pour on milk and stir well. Return to pan. Bring to the boil and cook for two minutes, stirring well.

3. Remove crusts from bread and crumble into custard. Stir in nuts. Allow to cool.

4. Whip cream to soft peaks and fold into cold custard.

5. Whisk egg whites to stiff peaks and fold in. Pour into serving dishes. Chill for 1 hour.

Each portion contains 10g CHO and 260 calories.

Note: This recipe is *not* suitable for freezing.

A special occasion tea: Kebabs (page 46) with salad and Rhubarb
Crumble Top (page 77).

A vegetarian meal: one piece of Lentil Bean Loaf (page 61) with salad and beans and an Apple and Blackberry Packet (page 76).

Apricot Queen of Puddings

Serves 4   Total CHO — 80g   Total Cals — 830

1 pint (550ml) semi-skimmed milk
1 oz (25g) polyunsaturated margarine
Rind and juice of 1 lemon
2 size 3 eggs, separated
4 oz (100g) wholemeal bread crumbs
4 oz (100g) fresh apricots, sliced
A few toasted almonds

1. Place milk, margarine and lemon rind in a saucepan, bring to the boil, remove from heat and leave to cool.

2. Once *cold*, squeeze in lemon juice, and beat in egg yolks.

3. Place breadcrumbs in the base of a flameproof dish. Pour on egg mixture. Bake at 350°F/180°C (Gas Mark 4) for 20 minutes or until set.

4. Place apricot slices on top. Whisk egg whites to stiff peaks and spread over apricots. Sprinkle with almonds.

5. Bake at 400°F/200°C (Gas Mark 6) for 15 minutes or until golden.

Each portion contains 20g CHO and 210 calories.

Note: This recipe is *not* suitable for freezing.

Bread Pudding

Slices into 12   Total CHO — 340g   Total Cals — 2360

6 oz (175g) crustless wholemeal bread
½ pint (275ml) semi-skimmed milk
12 oz (350g) mixed dried fruit
1 medium cooking apple, grated
3 tablespoons reduced-sugar marmalade
2 size 3 eggs, beaten
1 teaspoon lemon juice
1 teaspoon ground cinnamon
4 oz (100g) polyunsaturated margarine

1. Crumble bread into milk and leave for 45 minutes or until milk is absorbed.
2. Stir in fruit, grated apple, marmalade, eggs, lemon juice and cinnamon. Stir well.
3. Melt margarine, pour half into mixture and stir well. Pour mixture into a lightly-oiled 1 lb (450g) loaf tin.
4. Pour on remaining margarine.
5. Bake at 300°F/150°C (Gas Mark 2) for 1½ hours. Increase temperature to 350°F/180°C (Gas Mark 4) for 30 minutes. Serve hot with custard or cold as a cake.

Each piece contains 30g CHO and 195 calories.

Note: This recipe is *not* suitable for freezing.

Apricot Cream

Serves 5   Total CHO — 50g   Total Cals — 1100

1 lb (450g) fresh apricots
1 sachet gelatine
¼ pint (150ml) unsweetened orange juice
½ pint (275ml) whipping cream

1. Skin, halve and stone the apricots. Stew in a little water until tender.
2. Purée apricots. Mix gelatine into 2 tablespoons of boiling water. Beat into apricots.
3. Stir orange juice into mixture — leave to set.
4. Once apricots are on point of setting, whip cream to stiff peaks, whisk apricot mixture until foamy and fold cream in gently.
5. Pour into a serving dish and leave to set.

Each portion contains 10g CHO and 220 calories.

Note: This recipe is *not* suitable for freezing.

5. Special Occasions

More than 20 recipes to help with Special Occasions, Parties and Birthdays have been discussed in Chapter 1 and Christmas can, of course, be treated in the same way. Whilst at the BDA I wrote a leaflet entitled 'Christmas Cookery' in 1985 which may also prove useful.

Travelling and holidays with diabetic children may seem daunting but need cause no special problems — so long as you are prepared. Trains, planes, buses and boats get held up often, and cars get stuck in traffic, so always take food for snacks and meals that are even 8-10 hours away. Even if you do find refreshments at an airport or station, they may well not be entirely suitable! My diabetic sister spent 8 hours at Frankfurt Airport with only sweetened orange juice, cottage cheese, and cherry Danish pastries to keep her going — not exactly ideal.

If you are holidaying abroad, it is worth taking some familiar snack foods with you and if possible some 'diet' drinks — to save carrying large bottles of diet drink, take concentrates for a 'soda machine' and dilute with mineral water once on holiday. Many countries do sell these products but it could take you a little while to find them. Remember to take lots of insulin/blood-testing supplies, etc, and to ensure you have adequate holiday insurance.

Having said all of this, many diabetic families travel very successfully and *enjoy* themselves! Also it is important to remember that there are diabetic people abroad too so they do know what we are talking about!

Happy holidaying!

Cheesy Apricots

Serves 3   Total CHO — 30   Total Cals — 160

1 × 10 oz (285g) tin apricots in natural juice
5 oz (150g) 1 per cent fromage frais
1 sachet gelatine
2 tablespoons boiling water

1. Drain fruit, reserving juice. Place fruit in base of serving dish.
2. Mix fruit juice and fromage frais. Make up to 1 pint (550ml) with cold water.
3. Dissolve gelatine in boiling water and stir into fromage mixture. Pour over fruit and leave in a cool place to set.

Each portion contains 10g CHO and 55 calories.

Note: This recipe is *not* suitable for freezing.

Fruit on a Skewer
You will need 4 long skewers

Serves 4   Total CHO — 40g   Total Cals — 140

---

4 oz (100g) fresh apricots, in quarters or 4 dried apricots, soaked (6)
1 medium banana — sliced (15)
8 strawberries (6)
8 cubes of pineapple in natural juice (10)
Juice of a lemon

1. Divide fruit into 4 equal piles.
2. Coat banana well in lemon juice.
3. Thread alternating pieces of fruit onto skewers so that each has an equal share of fruit. Serve.

Each kebab contains 10g CHO and 35 calories.

Note: This recipe is *not* suitable for freezing. The figures shown in brackets are the approximate carbohydrate values of each fruit so that you can swap the fruits depending on the season.

Baked Custard

Serves 4   Total CHO 20g   Total Cals 340

*¾ pint (425ml) semi-
skimmed milk
2 size 3 eggs, beaten
A few drops of vanilla
essence*

1. Heat the milk but do not allow to boil.
Add beaten eggs and vanilla essence.
2. Pour into an ovenproof dish. Bake at
300°F/150°C (Gas Mark 2) for 1 hour.
Serve hot or cold.

Each portion contains 5g CHO and 85
calories.

Note: This recipe is *not* suitable for
freezing.

Prune Soufflé

Serves 6   Total CHO — 70g   Total Cals — 320

*6 oz (175g) stoned
prunes
½ pint (275ml) hot
tea
Zest of 1 lemon
4 size 3 egg whites*

1. Soak prunes in tea and lemon zest for
3 hours. Drain, reserving tea.
2. Purée prunes with 2 tablespoons of the
tea.
3. Whisk egg whites to stiff peaks. Gently
fold into prunes. Pour in a soufflé dish.
4. Bake at 350°F/180°C (Gas Mark 4) for
25 minutes. Serve immediately.

Each portion contains about 10g CHO
and 55 calories.

Note: This recipe is *not* suitable for
freezing.

Cashew Ice Cream
A rich dessert for special occasions

Serves 5   Total CHO — 50g   Total Cals — 750

---

4 oz (100g) unsalted cashew nuts
4 oz (100g) cottage cheese
1 tablespoon honey
¼ pint (150ml) water
2 size 3 egg whites

1. Blend nuts, cheese, honey and water until smooth (a food processor is the easiest way).
2. Whisk whites to stiff peaks.
3. Gently fold whites into nut mixture. Pour into a large bowl and freeze.
4. As the mixture freezes, stir twice.
5. Once frozen, process once more, serve or place in a covered container to freeze.
6. Allow to thaw for 10 minutes before serving from frozen.

Each portion contains 10g CHO and 150 calories.

Pear Hedgehogs

Serves 2   Total CHO — 10g   Total Cals — 40

---

2 pear halves, fresh or tinned in natural juice
Handful toasted almonds
4 raisins

1. Place pears flat side down on a plate.
2. Stick in almonds to represent spikes and raisins for eyes.
3. Chill and serve.

Each hedgehog contains 5g CHO and 20 calories.

Note: This recipe is *not* suitable for freezing.

Individual Sponge Puddings

Makes 6   Total CHO — 50g   Total Cals — 1030

3 oz (75g) wholemeal
self-raising flour
¾ teaspoon baking
powder
3 oz (75g)
polyunsaturated
margarine
1 oz (25g) fructose
2 size 3 eggs

1. Place all ingredients in a bowl and beat well together (a food processor works well here).

2. Spoon into 6 lightly oiled dariole moulds or madeleine tins — they should only be half full.

3. Bake at 350°F/180°C (Gas Mark 4) for 10-15 minutes or until risen and golden.

4. Remove from tins. Serve with custard, Carob Sauce (page 90) or fruit purée — remember to add accompaniment figures to those for your puddings.

Each pudding contains almost 10g CHO and 170 calories.

Note: This recipe freezes well.

Pears and Carob Sauce

Serves 4   Total CHO — 45g   Total Cals — 220

4 pear halves, fresh or tinned in natural juice
1 dessertspoon carob powder
1 dessertspoon cornflour
¼ pint (150ml) semi-skimmed milk

1. Place pear halves in serving dishes and chill.

2. Blend carob powder and cornflour with 2 tablespoons of milk.

3. Bring remaining milk to the boil, pour on to carob. Stir well.

4. Return to pan and, stirring continuously, bring to the boil. Simmer for two minutes.

5. Pour over pears and serve.

Each portion, i.e., 1 pear half and sauce, contains about 10g CHO and 55 calories.

Note: This recipe is *not* suitable for freezing.

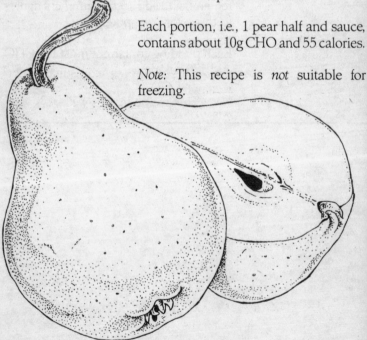

Carob Cream

Serves 4   Total CHO — 40g   Total Cals — 1120

½ pint (275ml) semi-
skimmed milk
½ oz (15g) cornflour
1 tablespoon carob
powder
½ teaspoon instant
coffee
½ pint (275ml)
whipping cream

1. Blend 2 tablespoons of the milk with the cornflour, carob and coffee.
2. Heat remaining milk to boiling point and pour on to carob mixture stirring well.
3. Return mixture to pan. Stirring all the time, heat to boiling, reduce heat and simmer for 2 minutes. Allow to cool.
4. Whip cream to stiff peaks. Fold into carob mixture and pour into serving dishes. Chill for 1 hour.

Each portion contains 10g CHO and 280 calories.

Note: This recipe is *not* suitable for freezing.

Strawberry Treat

Serves 3   Total CHO — 30g   Total Cals — 275

---

5 oz (150g) cottage
cheese
Grated zest and juice
of 1 orange
¾ lb (350g)
strawberries, cleaned

1. Rub the cottage cheese through a sieve. Add the grated zest and juice of orange and stir.
2. Chop all but 3 of the strawberries and stir into cheese.
3. Pour into 3 glasses and top with reserved fruit.

Each treat contains 10g CHO and 90 calories.

Note: This recipe is *not* suitable for freezing.

Cheese Straws
A party snack

| Makes 30 | Total CHO — 65g | Total Cals — 890 |

---

4 oz (100g)
wholemeal flour
Pinch of salt
2 oz (50g)
polyunsaturated
margarine
2 oz (50g) strong
cheese, grated
2 teaspoons cold
water

1. Beat all ingredients together (a food processor is ideal). Chill for 10 minutes.
2. Roll out to a rectangle ¼ inch (6mm) thick. Cut into 30 equal-size straw shapes.
3. Transfer to a lightly oiled baking tray.
4. Bake at 350°F/180°C (Gas Mark 4) for 5–7 minutes. Allow to cool on a wire rack.

10 straws contain 20g CHO and 300 calories.

Note: This recipe freezes well RAW.

Carob Crunchies

| Makes 10 | Total CHO — 50g | Total Cals — 690 |

---

2 oz (50g) (All Bran)
1 oz (25g) chopped
nuts
1 oz (25g) raisins
2 oz (50g)
polyunsaturated
margarine
1 tablespoon carob
powder

1. Mix *All Bran*, nuts and fruit well.
2. Melt margarine and stir in carob. Pour over bran mixture and stir well.
3. Spoon into paper cases and chill for 1 hour.

Each crunchie contains 5g CHO and 70 calories.

Note: This recipe is *not* suitable for freezing.

Chicken Quiche

Serves 6   Total CHO — 135g   Total Cals — 1660

Pastry
3 oz (75g)
polyunsaturated
margarine
6 oz (175g)
wholemeal flour
Cold water

Filling
8 oz (225g) cooked
chicken, chopped
3 oz (75g) mushrooms
1 onion, chopped
1 oz (25g) sweetcorn
2 size 3 eggs
⅓ pint (200ml) milk
Salt and pepper

1. Prepare pastry in the usual way, i.e., rub fat into flour and bring to a soft dough with cold water. (Food processors make excellent wholemeal pastry).

2. Roll out and line a 9 inch (23cm) flan dish. Chill for 10 minutes.

3. Bake blind at 400°F/200°C (Gas Mark 6) for 15 minutes. Allow to cool.

4. Place chicken and vegetables in base of flan case. Beat eggs in milk, season and pour over chicken and vegetables.

5. Bake at 400°F/200°C (Gas Mark 6) for 20–25 minutes or until set and golden. Serve hot or cold.

Each portion contains about 20g CHO and 275 calories.

Note: This recipe freezes well.

Vegetable Fingers

Use these as snacks or to accompany the dips on pages 95-7 for parties and picnics

---

Serves 4-6   Total CHO — 10g   Total Cals — 70

---

6 spring onions (2)
½ small cauliflower
(2)
1 green pepper (2)
3 oz (75g) mushrooms
(neg)
¼ cucumber (neg)
3 medium carrots (5)

1. Wash and prepare each vegetable, i.e., remove outer leaves or peel as appropriate.
2. Cut into equal sized 'fingers', arrange on a plate around a bowl of dip.

Each portion contains negligible CHO and 20-25 calories.

Note: This recipe is not suitable for freezing. The numbers in brackets show the approximate carbohydrate contents of each vegetable so that you can swap according to season.

Tuna Dip

Serve with Chicken Nuggets (page 58) or Vegetable Fingers (above)

Total CHO — negligible   Total Cals — 300

---

1 × 7 oz (200g) tin
tuna in brine,
drained and flaked
3 tablespoons low-fat
natural yogurt
¼ cucumber, chopped

1. Mix all ingredients well, and chill for 20 minutes.

Note: This recipe is not suitable for freezing.

Onion Dip

Serve with Chicken Nuggets (page 58) or Vegetable Fingers (page 95)

Total CHO — negligible   Total Cals — 150

---

4 oz (100g) skimmed-
    milk soft cheese
2 tablespoons low-fat
    natural yogurt
2 rings of green
    pepper, chopped
2 spring onions,
    chopped
1 clove of garlic,
    crushed (optional)

1. Mix all ingredients well. Chill for 20 minutes.

Note: This recipe is *not* suitable for freezing.

Peanut Dip

Lovely served with Chicken Nuggets (page 58) or Vegetable Fingers (page 95)

Total CHO — 5g	Total Cals 290

4 oz (100g) skimmed-milk soft cheese
3 tablespoons Peanut Butter (page 34)
2 tablespoons low-fat natural yogurt

1. Mix all ingredients well, and chill for 20 minutes.

Note: This recipe is *not* suitable for freezing.

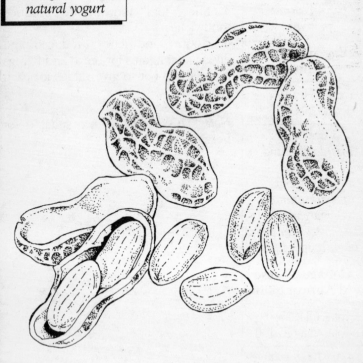

Rainbow Sandwiches
A change from ordinary sandwiches for your parties

Bread Total CHO — 370g   Bread Total Cals — 2320

1 small wholemeal loaf, uncut — approx 14 oz (400g)
1 small white loaf, uncut — approx 14 oz (400g)
3 oz (75g) polyunsaturated margarine

Egg and Ham Filling

Total CHO — neg
Total Cals — 500

3 size 3 eggs, hardboiled and mashed
1 oz (25g) polyunsaturated margarine
2 oz (50g) lean boiled ham, chopped finely

Cottage Cheese and Apricot Filling

Total CHO — 5g
Total Cals — 100

4 oz (100g) cottage cheese

1. Mix ingredients for each filling well. Chill for 10 minutes.
2. Cut the crusts from each loaf. Slice each loaf *horizontally* into 4. Using alternate slices of white and brown, reform a double size loaf using margarine and a layer of different fillings.
3. Slice 'loaf' *vertically* to produce sandwiches.
4. Count sandwiches produced and divide total figures for bread and fillings by this number to give values for each sandwich.

Note: This recipe is *not* suitable for freezing.

½ oz (15g) dried
apricots, soaked and
chopped finely

**Cheese, Apple and
Peanut Filling**

Total CHO — 25g
Total Cals — 490

4 oz (100g) hard
cheese, grated
2 eating apples,
chopped
2 tablespoons of
Peanut Butter
(page 34)

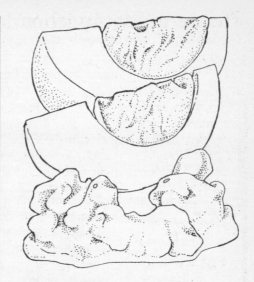

Cheesy Corn Fritters

Makes 8 Total CHO — 85g Total Cals — 700

3 tablespoons
wholemeal flour
1 teaspoon baking
powder
Pinch of salt
6 oz (175g) sweetcorn
2 size 3 eggs,
separated
1 × 5 oz (150g)
carton cottage cheese
3 tablespoons semi-
skimmed milk
A little vegetable oil

1. Mix flour, baking powder, salt and sweetcorn.
2. Stir in egg yolks, cheese and milk.
3. Whisk egg whites until stiff, fold into mixture.
4. Heat oil in a heavy based pan. Spoon mixture into small circles and fry for 5 minutes each side.
5. Serve warm.

Each fritter contains 10g CHO and 90 calories.

Note: This recipe is *not* suitable for freezing.

Home-made Lemonade
A refreshing change to lots of colourings and sweeteners

Makes 2 pints (1100ml)
Total CHO — 20g   Total Cals — 70

---

*Zest and juice of 2
large lemons
2 pints (1100ml)
boiling water
1 tablespoon honey*

1. Place zest and juice into a large mixing bowl. Pour on boiling water.
2. Stir in honey and leave to stand until completely cold (at least 3 hours).
3. Strain out peel. Pour lemonade into a large empty bottle to store.
4. Before serving, sweeten to taste if necessary with artificial calorie-free sweetener, and water down if necessary for young children.

Note: This recipe is *not* suitable for freezing, but will keep for 1 week in the fridge.

6. *Menu Suggestions*

Some menu suggestions for you to fit into your child's allowance and your family's eating habits.

MENU 1
A lunch with 30g CHO and 360 calories

	CHO	Cals
1 Quarky Peanut Butter Open Sandwich (pages 32-3) — 1 slice of bread	15g	260
1 Doughnut (page 41)	10g	80
½ apple, sliced	5g	20
	30g	360

MENU 2
A packed lunch with 40g CHO and 295 calories

	CHO	Cals
1 Chilli Beef Pancake Parcel (pages 27 and 30)	15g	150
1 Crumpet (page 39)	20g	125
Fresh fruit	5g	20
1 diet drink	—	—
	40g	295

MENU 3
A morning snack for school with 20g CHO and 120 calories

	CHO	Cals
2 Muesli Drops (page 70)	10g	80
1 banana	10g	40
	20g	120

MENU 4

A bedtime snack with 20g CHO and 235 calories

	CHO	Cals
1 piece of Kolac (page 71)	10g	105
1 glass whole milk	10g	130
	20g	235

MENU 5

A weekend lunch in a hurry! 40g CHO and 350 calories

	CHO	Cals
1 Home-made Burger (page 45)	—	115
1 Home-made Roll (page 35)	30g	155
1 diet yogurt	10g	80
	40g	350

MENU 6

An evening meal with 50g CHO and 395 calories

	CHO	Cals
1 piece of Ham Pizza (page 25)	30g	175
Green salad	—	10
1 portion Apricot Queen of Puddings (page 81)	20g	210
	50g	395

MENU 7

A special occasion tea with 60g CHO and 590 calories

	CHO	Cals
Salad (with 1 oz (25g) beans added)	5g	45
1 Kebab (page 46)	neg	140
1 Home-made Roll (page 35)	30g	155
1 piece Rhubarb Crumble Top (page 77)	25g	250
	60g	590

MENU 8

A vegetarian meal with 40g CHO and 515 calories

	CHO	Cals
1 piece of Lentil Bean Loaf (page 61)	20g	130
1 portion of salad (with 1 oz (25g) beans added)	5g	45
1 Apple and Blackberry Packet (page 76)	15g	340
	40g	515

Recommended Reading

These books contain useful information and many recipes suitable for children.

Countdown
(Published by British Diabetic Association)
A guide to the carbohydrate and calorie content of manufactured foods.

Better Cookery for Diabetics
(Published by British Diabetic Association)
A recipe book by Jill Metcalfe.

Simple Home Baking
(Published by British Diabetic Association)
A recipe leaflet by Sue Hall.

The Diabetic's Microwave Cookbook
(Published by Thorsons Publishing Group, 1986)
A microwave book by Sue Hall.

The Diabetes Handbook — Insulin Dependent Diabetes
(Published by Thorsons Publishing Group, 1986)
By Dr John Day.

Packed Lunches and Snacks
(Published by Thorsons Publishing Group, 1986)
A recipe book by Sue Hall.

Good Food — Healthy Children
(Published by Conran Octopus, 1986)
A book for children by Gail Duff. Not a diabetic book but full of good advice.

School Pack
(Published by the British Diabetic Association)

Christmas Cookery
(Published by the British Diabetic Association, 1985)
A recipe leaflet by Sue Hall.

Appendix: List of Food Values

The carbohydrate and calorie contents of all the ingredients mentioned in the book are given so you can swap foods around and do a little experimenting of your own.

Food	Amount	gCHO	Cals
Apple — eating, whole	1	10	40
— cooking as bought	1 lb (450g)	35	140
Apricots — fresh	1 lb (450g)	28	125
— tinned in natural juice	1×14 oz (410g)	40	190
— dried, stoned	1 oz (25g)	12	50
Arrowroot	1 oz (25g)	27	100
Banana — peeled	1 small	10	40
Beans — Borlotti, tinned	1×15 oz (425g) tin	40	250
— red kidney, tinned	1×15 oz (425g) tin	64	330
— baked in tomato sauce	1 oz (25g)	3	20
Beansprouts, raw	1 lb (450g)	10	50
Blackberries — as bought	1 lb (450g)	30	130
Bread — wholemeal	1oz (25g)	12	60
— white	1 oz (25g)	15	65
Breadcrumbs	1 oz (25g)	12	60
Cabbage	1 lb (450g)	15	100
Carrot — raw	1 lb (450g)	20	90
Carob	1 oz (25g)	10	50
Cashew nuts	1 oz (25g)	7	140
Cauliflower — raw	1 lb (450g)	6	50
Cheese — Cheddar type	1 oz (25g)	neg	115
— cottage	1 oz (25g)	neg	27

— skimmed-milk soft	1 oz (25g)	neg	40
Chicken — white meat	1 lb (450g)	—	540
Coconut — desiccated	1 oz (25g)	1	170
Cornflour	1 oz (25g)	25	90
Courgette — raw	1 lb (450g)	15	100
Cream — whipping	1 oz (25g)	½	80
Cucumber	1 lb (450g)	8	45
Custard powder	1 oz (25g)	26	100
Dates — stoned, dried	1 oz (25g)	18	70
Eggs, size 3 — raw	1	neg	75
Fish — fillet, white, raw	1 lb (450g)	neg	345
Flour — wholemeal plain/ self-raising	1 oz (25g)	18	90
— white plain/ self-raising	1 oz (25g)	22	100
— 81 per cent	1 oz (25g)	19	92
Fromage frais (1 per cent)	1 oz (25g)	neg	15
Fructose	1 oz (25g)	30*	115
Gelatine	1 sachet	neg	35
Ham — lean, boiled	1 oz (25g)	neg	35
Honey — clear	1 oz (25g)	20	80
Jam — reduced-sugar	1 oz (25g)	8–10	30
Leeks — raw	1 lb (450g)	30	140
Lemon — raw	1	neg	10
Lentils — raw, all types	1 oz (25g)	15	85
Macaroni — wholewheat	1 oz (25g)	19	95
Mandarins — tinned in natural juice	1×10 oz (300g) can	25	100
Margarine—polyunsaturated	1 oz (25g)	neg	210
Mayonnaise — reduced oil	1 tablespoon	neg	35
Milk — semi-skimmed	1 pint (550ml)	30	260
Mince — beef, lean	1 lb (450g)	neg	820
Mushrooms — raw	1 lb (450g)	neg	70
Nuts — any variety	1 oz (25g)	2–5	10
Oats/Oatmeal — raw	1 oz (25g)	20	110
Oil — vegetable	1 fl oz (30ml)	neg	255

Onion — raw	1 lb (450g)	25	100
Orange juice — unsweetened	¼ pint (150ml)	15	60
Parsnips — raw, as bought	1 lb (450g)	40	160
Peanuts — shelled	1 oz (25g)	2	160
Pears — eating	1 large	10	40
Peas — green	1 oz (25g)	3	20
Peppers — any colour, raw	1 lb (450g)	8	60
Pilchards — tinned	1×15 oz (425g)	neg	500
Pineapple — tinned in juice	1×15oz (425g)	55	240
Plums — eating, raw	1 lb (450g)	40	160
Pork — lean	1 lb (450g)	neg	600
Potatoes — raw	1 lb (450g)	80	340
Prunes — fresh	1 lb (450g)	150	600
— tinned in natural juice	15 oz (425g) tin	68	270
Raisins	1 oz (25g)	18	70
Rhubarb	1 lb (450g)	5	30
Rice — brown	1 oz (25g)	20	95
Salami	1 oz (25g)	neg	140
Sausagemeat	1 lb (450g)	45	1575
Strawberries	1 lb (450g)	27	110
Sultanas	1 oz (25g)	18	70
Sweetcorn	1×11 oz (133g) tin	55	250
Tomatoes — tinned	1×14oz (405g)	10	50
Tuna — in brine	1×7 oz (200g) tin	—	220
Vegetable fat — white	1 oz (25g)	—	255
Yogurt — low-fat natural	1×5 oz (150g)	10	80

* note usually ignored if less than 1 oz (25g) taken in one day.

Further Information

BRITISH DIABETIC ASSOCIATION

Diabetes affects just over two per cent of the UK population. Although it cannot be cured or prevented, it can be controlled by proper treatment.

The *British Diabetic Association* (BDA) was formed in 1934 to help all diabetics to overcome prejudice and ignorance about diabetes, and to raise money for research. The Association is currently budgeting over £1.5m each year to treat, prevent or cure diabetes, and is the largest single contributor to diabetic research in the UK.

The Association is an independent organization with over 100,000 members and 350 local branches. It provides information and advice for diabetics and their families. It also liaises closely with those who work in the field of diabetes.

Education and activity holidays are organized for diabetics of all ages plus teach-in weekends for families with diabetic children or teenagers.

The BDA's bi-monthly magazine *Balance* keeps readers up to date with news of the latest research and all aspects of diabetes. It is sent free to members or available from local newsagents, price 85p.

All diabetics have to follow a lifelong diet and *Balance* publishes recipes and dietary information to help bring interest and variety to eating.

To become a member, fill in the application form and send it with your subscription to:

British Diabetic Association,
10 Queen Anne Street,
London W1M 0BD.
Tel: 01-323 1531

Enrolment Form

The British Diabetic Association
10 Queen Anne Street
London W1M 0BD

MEMBERSHIP SUBSCRIPTIONS

Life membership	Single payment of £175 or £25 a year for 7 years under covenant
Annual membership	£7.50 a year
Reduced Membership — pensioner, student on Government grant and those in receipt of DHSS benefits	£2.00 a year
Overseas annual membership	£10.00 a year
Overseas life membership	Single payment of £150.00

Please enrol me as a:

☐ Life member: £175 £25 a year for 7 years under covenant

☐ Annual member: £7.50

☐ Pensioner member: £2.00

☐ Overseas annual member: £10.00

☐ Overseas Life member: £150.00

☐ Are you joining on behalf of a child?

I enclose Remittance/Banker's Order for £ ....
(Please delete whichever does not apply)

Date .... Signature ....

Full name: Mr/Mrs/Miss ....
(Block Capitals please)

Address ....
....

Date of Birth .... Occupation ....
(This information will be treated as strictly confidential)

Index